Wordsworth and Coleridge

Lyrical Ballads

Edited by Celia de Piro

Oxford University Press

OXFORD
UNIVERSITY PRESS

Great Clarendon Street, Oxford OX2 6DP

Oxford University Press is a department of the University of Oxford.
It furthers the University's objective of excellence in research, scholarship,
and education by publishing worldwide in

Oxford   New York

Auckland   Cape Town   Dar es Salaam   Hong Kong   Karachi
Kuala Lumpur   Madrid   Melbourne   Mexico City   Nairobi
New Delhi   Shanghai   Taipei   Toronto

With offices in

Argentina   Austria   Brazil   Chile   Czech Republic   France   Greece
Guatemala   Hungary   Italy   Japan   South Korea   Poland   Portugal
Singapore   Switzerland   Thailand   Turkey   Ukraine   Vietnam

Oxford is a registered trade mark of Oxford University Press
in the UK and in certain other countries

British Library Cataloguing in Publication Data
Data available

ISBN-13: 978-019-832547-5

3 5 7 9 10 8 6 4 2

Typeset in Goudy Old Style MT
by Palimpsest Book Production Limited, Grangemouth, Stirlingshire

Printed and bound in Great Britain by Cox and Wyman Ltd., Reading

The Publishers would like to thank the following for permission to reproduce
photographs: p3t Hulton Archive/Getty Images; p4b The Bridgeman Art Library; p7 The
Wordsworth Trust; p137 Archivo Iconografico, S.A./Corbis UK Ltd; p178 The Wordsworth
Trust; The illustration on p126 is by Martin Cottam.

Contents

Editors

Celia de Piro was born and educated in Yorkshire. After reading English she was awarded the Wordsworth Research Fellowship at St Hugh's College, Oxford, where she spent some years in research and teaching. She has since been a senior lecturer in a college of education, a tutor for the Open University and an A-level examiner. For many years she taught English at Cheltenham Ladies' College. Publications include works of criticism, biography and poetry.

Dr Victor Lee, the series editor, read English at University College, Cardiff. He was later awarded his doctorate at the University of Oxford. He has taught at secondary and tertiary level, working at the Open University for 27 years. Victor Lee's experience as an examiner is very wide. He has been, for example, a Chief Examiner in English A level for three different boards, stretching over a period of more than 30 years.

Foreword

Oxford Student Texts are specifically aimed at presenting poetry and drama to an audience studying English literature at an advanced level. Each text is designed as an integrated whole consisting of four main parts. The first part sets the scene by discussing the context in which the work was written. The most important part of the book is the poetry or play itself, and it is suggested that the student read this first without consulting the Notes or other secondary sources. To encourage students to follow this advice, the Notes are placed together after the text, not alongside it. Where help is needed, the Notes and Interpretations sections provide it.

The Notes perform two functions. First, they provide information and explain allusions. Second (this is where they differ from most texts at this level), they often raise questions of central concern to the interpretation of the poems or play being dealt with, particularly in the general note placed at the beginning of each set of notes.

The fourth part, the Interpretations section, deals with major issues of response to the particular selection of poetry or drama. One of the major aims of this part of the text is to emphasize that there is no one right answer to interpretation, but a series of approaches. Readers are given guidance as to what counts as evidence, but in the end left to make up their own minds as to which are the most suitable interpretations, or to add their own.

In these revised editions, the Interpretations section now addresses a wider range of issues. There is a more detailed treatment of context and critical history, for example. The section contains a number of activity-discussion sequences, although it must be stressed that these are optional. Significant issues about the poetry or play are raised, and readers are invited to tackle activities before proceeding to the discussion section, where possible responses to the questions raised are considered. Their main function is to engage readers actively in the ideas of the text.

At the end of each text there is also a list of Essay Questions. Whereas the activity-discussion sequences are aimed at increasing understanding of the literary work itself, these tasks are intended to help explore ideas about the poetry or play after the student has completed the reading of the work and the studying of the Notes and Interpretations. These tasks are particularly helpful for coursework projects or in preparation for an examination.

Victor Lee
Series Editor

List of Abbreviations

The major texts referred to in this edition are the following:

BL *Biographia Literaria,* ed. H. Nelson Coleridge, Bell & Sons, London, 1898.

Letters *Collected Letters of Samuel Taylor Coleridge,* ed. E.L. Griggs, Oxford University Press, 1956–1971, six volumes.

Notebooks *Collected Notebooks of Samuel Taylor Coleridge,* ed. Kathleen Coburn, Routledge & Kegan Paul, 1957–

Fenwick Notes (notes on his poems dictated by Wordsworth to Isabella Fenwick) *The Fenwick Notes of William Wordsworth,* ed. Jared Curtis, Bristol Classical Press, 1993.

Note

Footnotes marked with an asterisk in *Lyrical Ballads* are the poets' own comments. Editorial footnotes are numbered throughout the text.

Lyrical Ballads in Context

On 5 June 1797, Samuel Taylor Coleridge, then aged 25, vaulted over a gate which afforded a short cut to Racedown Lodge in Dorset where William Wordsworth and his sister Dorothy were tenants. Dorothy never forgot the dramatic effect of her first view of Coleridge in his eagerness to join his friends. The act was typical of his impetuous nature. Having met briefly in 1795, neither poet could have dreamed that they were about to begin a remarkable literary friendship, and that its first fruits would be this little volume, experimental in kind, but marking an end in literature to the eighteenth-century age of taste and refinement. *Lyrical Ballads* would define an age of sensibility rather than reason, setting free an imaginative energy we now call the Romantic Movement.

It was not a sudden discovery of the romantic spirit, but in English poetry it was a major change of emphasis, style and subject. Moreover *Lyrical Ballads* contains two masterpieces: *The Rime of the Ancyent Marinere* and *Lines Written a Few Miles above Tintern Abbey*. It marks a meeting of two very different artists and men. Part of your textual study will be to explore how these poems are a blending of their two voices. In your reading of the Preface of 1800 (reprinted as an Appendix on pp. 227–44), in which Wordsworth attempted to justify these *experiments*, you will have an opportunity to reflect on how Wordsworth and Coleridge were breaking free from the rigid metres and artificial figures of speech of the previous century, establishing a new conception of the role of the poet. Judging how far they succeeded will be your final task.

The following approaches may be helpful. Remember that these are of *equal* value, and that your final appreciation should be essentially your own study of form, language and ideas, bearing in mind that the poets were working in a new literary medium.

- Keep in mind the historical and cultural background to these poems, for they were written in a dramatic period immediately after the French Revolution. England was at war with France and the Industrial Revolution was beginning to have serious social repercussions.

- Consider the different backgrounds and characters of the poets, because their understanding of Romanticism was not the same.

- Study the section entitled Interpretations, which will help you to understand how the work of these two poets was received by contemporary critics and how later generations viewed it.

- Look at the longer perspective in order to decide whether *Lyrical Ballads* was truly revolutionary or just a group of homely tales lamenting lost innocence.

On their first meeting Coleridge stayed for two weeks! Look at the portraits opposite. Coleridge was *a noticeable man with large grey eyes*. Wordsworth thought him *the most wonderful man I ever knew*, and by this he meant literally a man full of *wonder*. Wordsworth fulfilled the stereotype of a true northerner, never really happy away from his native Lake District. With his stern, profile he seemed *a sadder and a wiser man*. The young William Hazlitt, a regular visitor at this time, disliked Wordsworth's brooding nature, believing that Coleridge looked and sounded more than any man he had ever seen like his idea of a genius.

Coleridge's intellect was like a flash of lightning, but lightning is not a power easily harnessed. Wordsworth had something earthlike in his nature – not a bookish man like Coleridge, but a natural philosopher. In Coleridge, Wordsworth gained his greatest disciple. Wordsworth wanted to be an epic poet and Coleridge assured him that this was his destiny. Their meeting was a defining moment in both their lives. Each was strong where the other was weak. In 1798, Wordsworth was full of moral

The English Romantic poet William Wordsworth (1798).
(Photo: Hulton Archive/Getty Images)

Coleridge in Germany, an original pastel, 1799.
(Reproduced by kind permission of Mrs Gardner, Private Collection)

uncertainties but had a passionate faith in his own powers of vision. Coleridge possessed a brilliantly analytical mind, fortified by philosophy, and coupled with a deep Christian faith. These qualities bolstered Wordsworth's flagging faith in humanity, while Coleridge became more focused, eager to demonstrate his original views on the imagination and the role of the poet.

William Wordsworth, 1770–1850

Wordsworth was born on 7 April 1770 at Cockermouth in Cumberland, the son of the land agent to the Earl of Lonsdale. After a privileged beginning, the children were orphaned and, at the age of thirteen, William was boarded at Hawkshead Grammar School and Dorothy sent to live with an aunt. At school William enjoyed what seems to have been an idyllic country childhood. In October 1788 he went up to St John's College, Cambridge, but his mind was more on poetic *effusions* than his studies and, homesick for the lakes and hills of Cumberland, he made a trip to the Alps in 1790. In November 1791 Wordsworth left Cambridge altogether, journeying first to Paris where the ruins of the Bastille and the political upheaval made a deep impression on him. Here he fell in love with Annette Vallon, who bore him a daughter. His meeting with the soldier and patriot Michael Beaupuy was influential in consolidating his radical and republican views. (For Wordsworth's own account of this period see *The Prelude, Book V*.)

The September Massacres in Paris in 1792 caused Wordsworth to reflect on his political loyalties. In February 1793, France declared war on England and Holland. In the same year Louis XVI was executed, and between 1793 and 1794 a Reign of Terror leading to the guillotining of the French nobility plunged France into upheaval and Wordsworth into moral crisis. His love of justice and equality and his committed atheism were not easily uprooted. In 1793 Wordsworth wrote an essay on political theory in the form of an open letter to the Bishop of

Llandaff in which he spoke of the grievances of the labouring poor, especially hard in times of war, and the need to establish civil liberties. The letter is not theoretical but full of moral passion.

Wordsworth had become an ardent admirer of William Godwin's *Inquiry Concerning Political Justice* (1793). Godwin, like Thomas Paine (*Rights of Man*, 1791) had argued for the supremacy of reason over sentiment, for the abolition of marriage, for atheism, feminism and republicanism, but after first-hand experience of what happens to a society when it attempts violently to tear up its roots, Wordsworth now began to re-examine his moral conscience. In 1795 he returned to England, renting Racedown Lodge in Dorset with Dorothy, and there he suffered a form of nervous collapse. It was from this despondency that Coleridge's *capacious soul* and *influence of my heart of hearts* (*Prelude*, Book XIV, lines 266 and 291) rescued him in the summer of 1797. Wordsworth found Coleridge *wonderful in the power he possessed of throwing out in profusion grand central truths from which might be evolved the most comprehensive systems.* Within a month the Wordsworths moved to the manor house at Alfoxden, just four miles from Coleridge's cottage at Nether Stowey in Somerset. Coleridge's intellectual and moral dynamism, unchecked by any first-hand experience of the horrors of revolution, lifted Wordsworth's spirits and returned his mind to poetry.

Samuel Taylor Coleridge, 1772–1834

Born on 21 October 1772, Coleridge was the tenth child of the impoverished vicar of the church of Ottery St Mary in Devon. From his youth, his appetite for knowledge was insatiable, especially for myth, folklore, the supernatural, travel, mysticism and philosophy. This taste for obscure learning never left him. His mind *had been habituated to the Vast* (*Letters*, vol. I, p. 354) and this fever for some grand unifying design to the universe was to be his strength and his weakness. Coleridge's circumstances changed with the death of his father. In 1782 he gained a charity scholarship at Christ's Hospital, London, where he excelled in studying Classics. Homesick, lonely, usually left in the city for his summer holidays, he was driven to obsessive reading on the leads of the roof, *seeing nought lovely but the sky and stars* (*Frost at Midnight*, line 53).

From a stern Classics master, however, he learned a vital lesson: *that Poetry, even that of the loftiest and, seemingly, that of the wildest odes, had a logic of its own, as severe as that of science.* His earliest poetry shows an ability to write with *the lines running into each other, instead of closing at each couplet, and in a more natural language, neither bookish nor vulgar* (*Letters*, vol. I, p. 53). In 1791 Coleridge went up to Jesus College, Cambridge, but in December 1793, he abandoned academic life before taking his degree and, in a bout of patriotism, joined the 15th Light Dragoons. This lunatic episode was resolved only by purchasing his discharge. The regimental muster roll recorded the event succinctly: *10 April 1794. S.T. Coleridge: Discharged Insane.*

Coleridge next devised a political scheme with his fellow poet Robert Southey called Pantisocracy, a democratic social science based on the rules of nature to be established in a new community in New England. Needing a useful addition to the colonial enterprise, Coleridge acquired a wife, Southey's sister-in-law Sara Fricker – a union joined in October 1795 and soon regretted. Through the Pantisocratic scheme, which eventually collapsed for want of funds, Coleridge met many dissenting radicals, including the controversial republican John Thelwall, shortly to be tried for treason, and Thomas Poole, through whom he rented a cottage at Nether Stowey. Coleridge's son, named Hartley after the philosopher in whom he happened to be interested at the time, was born in 1796.

At this point Coleridge was leading a hectic life as a journalist for the radical magazine *The Watchman* as well as writing poetry, and in April 1796 he published his first volume of

51 poems, *Poems on Various Subjects*. Behind his radical views lay
a devout Christian faith and, as a Unitarian minister, he began a
preaching tour proposing advanced views on the slave trade,
capital, property and feminism. Hazlitt records his first memory
of Coleridge reading a section of the gospel describing Christ's
days in the wilderness: *And he went up into the mountain to pray,
himself, alone.* Hazlitt never forgot the profound and terrible
meaning the word *alone* seemed to signify in Coleridge's voice, a
word that would resound throughout his greatest poem *The Rime
of the Ancyent Marinere.*

Alfoxden House by J. MacWhirter. (The Wordsworth Trust)

7

The conception of *Lyrical Ballads*

And so in June 1797, Wordsworth, having lived for almost two years in seclusion, was admitted to a circle of radical thinkers committed to social reform. It was an intoxicating blend of idealism. Moreover, through Coleridge, he acquired the lease of Alfoxden House and the surrounding deer park. Here Wordsworth could lead the life of a literary gentleman and devote himself entirely to poetry.

Radicalism, though suitably gentrified, was not without its amusing side. One purchaser of *The Watchman* complained about the *seditious dog* who had composed the motto on the prospectus – *That all might know the truth, and that the truth may make us free* – learning to his confusion that it was none other than Jesus Christ! Thelwall's presence caused suspicion and a secret agent was sent from London to keep watch on the group's movements, reporting the inhabitants of Alfoxden House to be *a Sett of violent Democrats*. In fact, Thelwall, like Wordsworth, was in search of peace after an exhausting radical career in politics. Coleridge later recalled their conversation (July 1830):

> We were once sitting in a beautiful recess in the Quantocks, when I said to him 'Citizen John, this is a fine place to talk treason in.' 'Nay! Citizen Samuel!' replied he, 'it is rather a place to make a man forget that there is any necessity for treason!'

> *(The Table Talk and Omniana of S.T. Coleridge, with a note on Coleridge by Coventry Patmore,* Oxford University Press, 1917, p. 105)

One tragic development marked the end of that eventful year. During the summer, Coleridge began taking opium, initially for a painful tooth. During a walk in October he retired to a farmhouse in order to take an opiate to relieve his pain, after which he fell into a *reverie* during which the poem *Kubla Khan* 'appeared' to him. On awaking he copied down the poem almost like a dictation. The poem was to make literary history – a living example of his own theory of the imagination. (See *BL*, Ch. XIII and Interpretations, p. 198.) Sadly, this wonderful poem also marks the beginning of Coleridge's addiction to opium, a habit that was to wreck his life.

Lyrical Ballads did not become fully shaped until March 1798. Although written initially to raise 30 guineas for a walking tour of Germany, Wordsworth and Coleridge eagerly discussed the ballad form[1] as a fresh and original way of giving more human interest to the Romantic idea of nature. The volume would constitute a single work – a dramatic whole – combining the personal voice of the lyric with the plain narrative of the ballad. In May, Coleridge wrote to the publisher: *We deem that the volumes offered to you are to a certain degree one work, in kind tho' not in degree as an Ode is one work – and that our different poems are as stanzas* (*Letters*, vol. I, pp. 411–12). They would employ ordinary language to convey subtle moral truths. Wordsworth would attempt to describe ordinary people in homely settings under unusual stress. Coleridge would employ a more Gothic style in his ballad and a more lyric style in other poems. The work would be divided in the following way:

> ...my endeavors [Coleridge's] should be directed to persons and characters supernatural, or at least romantic; yet so as to transfer from our inward nature a human interest and a semblance of truth sufficient to procure from these shadows of imagination that willing suspension of disbelief for the moment, which constitutes poetic faith. Mr. Wordsworth's on the other hand, was to propose to himself as his object, to give the charm of novelty to things of every day, and to excite a feeling analogous to the supernatural, by awakening the mind's attention from the lethargy of custom, and directing it to the loveliness and the wonders of the world before us.
>
> (*BL*, Ch. XIV, see Appendices, p. 253)

---

[1] A ballad was originally a song incorporating a narrative or popular folk tale, and using refrains or repetitions in a rhythmical manner. It was much revived in the eighteenth century, particularly in Thomas Percy's *Reliques* (1765) and the work of Robert Burns (see, for example, the reference to Burns's *Tam o Shanter* in the Notes to *The Idiot Boy*, p. 164).

Both poets were aiming at the supernatural, yet the word did not mean the preternatural as in Gothic horror but rather a *visionary* quality presenting ordinary human experience in an unusual perspective. To this end, Coleridge was already writing *Christabel* and *The Dark Ladie*, neither of which he would finish even for the second edition. But their differences of philosophy soon surfaced. Coleridge was convinced that *no man was ever a great poet, without being at the same time a profound philosopher* (BL, Ch. XV, p. 155), yet Wordsworth knew little philosophy, proudly proclaiming that he had never read a word of German metaphysics *thank heaven!* Naturally contemplative, he was essentially anti-intellectual, interested neither in God nor redemption but in the world around him and how it reflected his own nature, an egoism that Coleridge felt to be *all male*. Hazlitt commented: *It is as if there were nothing but himself in the universe. He lives in the busy solitude of his own heart: in the deep silence of thought* (Hazlitt: Selected Writings, ed. R. Blyth, Penguin, 1970, p. 59).

Even in social terms Coleridge and Wordsworth were different. For most of his life Wordsworth would preside over a household of adoring women; Coleridge would suffer a broken marriage and spend much of his life alone, and his Mariner conveys his deepest fears. Living in the light of his own imagination and dreams, Coleridge was highly sensitive to everything around him, whereas Wordsworth was methodical and eager to gain a poetic reputation. Even the way they composed shows their differences:

> Coleridge liked to compose in walking over uneven ground, or breaking through the straggling branches of a copse wood... Wordsworth...walking up and down a straight gravel path, beating out the rhythm and repeating the lines to himself over and over.
>
> (*Hazlitt: Selected Writings*, pp. 59–60)

For Wordsworth, spontaneity was unimportant. Poetry needed to acquire an almost classical serenity. Hazlitt records Coleridge talking in the park at Alfoxden of their sense of a new style and a new spirit of poetry, yet regretting that Wordsworth was not interested in folklore or superstition attached to places:

> ...there was something corporeal, a matter of factness, a clinging to the palpable, or often the petty, in his poetry, in consequence. His genius...sprung out of the ground like a flower, or unfolded...itself from a green spray, on which the gold-finch sang...his soul seemed to inhabit the universe like a palace, and to discover truth by intuition, rather than by deduction.
>
> **(Hazlitt: Selected Writings, pp. 59–60)**

Because Wordsworth's name was relatively unknown and his own attached to radical views, Coleridge agreed that *Lyrical Ballads* would appear anonymously, *The Rime of the Ancyent Marinere* coming first, and Wordsworth's ode *Tintern Abbey* closing the volume. Though their views on the craft of poetry did not accord (we will continue this debate in the section entitled Interpretations), they were both passionate Romantics working together with an eager resolve to restore a sense of wonder and beauty to a violent world. By September 1798 *Lyrical Ballads* was with the publishers, and at the end of the month Wordsworth and Coleridge set sail for Germany.

Lyrical Ballads, with a Few Other Poems

Advertisement

It is the honourable characteristic of Poetry that its materials are to be found in every subject which can interest the human mind. The evidence of this fact is to be sought, not in the writings of Critics, but in those of Poets themselves.

The majority of the following poems are to be considered as experiments. They were written chiefly with a view to ascertain how far the language of conversation in the middle and lower classes of society is adapted to the purposes of poetic pleasure. Readers accustomed to the gaudiness and inane phraseology of many modern writers, if they persist in reading this book to its conclusion, will perhaps frequently have to struggle with feelings of strangeness and aukwardness: they will look round for poetry, and will be induced to enquire by what species of courtesy these attempts can be permitted to assume that title. It is desirable that such readers, for their own sakes, should not suffer the solitary word Poetry, a word of very disputed meaning, to stand in the way of their gratification; but that, while they are perusing this book, they should ask themselves if it contains a natural delineation of human passions, human characters, and human incidents; and if the answer be favorable to the author's wishes, that they should consent to be pleased in spite of that most dreadful enemy to our pleasures, our own pre-established codes of decision.

Readers of superior judgment may disapprove of the style in which many of these pieces are executed it must be expected that many lines and phrases will not exactly suit their taste. It will perhaps appear to them, that wishing to avoid the prevalent fault of the day, the author has sometimes descended too low, and that many of his expressions are too familiar, and not of sufficient dignity. It is apprehended, that the more conversant the reader is with our elder writers, and with those in modern times who have been the most successful in painting manners and passions, the fewer complaints of this kind will he have to make.

An accurate taste in poetry, and in all the other arts, Sir Joshua Reynolds has observed, is an acquired talent, which can only be produced by severe thought, and a long continued intercourse with the best models of composition. This is mentioned not with so ridiculous a purpose as to prevent the most inexperienced reader from judging for himself; but merely to temper the rashness of decision, and to suggest that if poetry be a subject on which much time has not been bestowed, the judgment may be erroneous, and that in many cases it necessarily will be so.

The tale of Goody Blake and Harry Gill is founded on a well-authenticated fact which happened in Warwickshire. Of the other poems in the collection, it may be proper to say that they are either absolute inventions of the author, or facts which took place within his personal observation or that of his friends. The poem of the Thorn, as the reader will soon discover, is not supposed to be spoken in the author's own person: the character of the loquacious narrator will sufficiently shew itself in the course of the story. The Rime of the Ancyent Marinere was professedly written in imitation of the *style*, as well as of the spirit of the elder poets; but with a few exceptions, the Author believes that the language adopted in it has been equally intelligible for these three last centuries. The lines entitled Expostulation and Reply, and those which follow, arose out of conversation with a friend who was somewhat unreasonably attached to modern books of moral philosophy.

The Rime of the Ancyent Marinere

in seven parts

ARGUMENT

How a Ship having passed the Line was driven by Storms to the cold Country towards the South Pole; and how from thence she made her course to the tropical Latitude of the Great Pacific Ocean; and of the strange things that befell; and in what manner the Ancyent Marinere came back to his own Country.

Part I

It is an ancyent Marinere,
    And he stoppeth one of three:
'By thy long grey beard and thy glittering eye
    'Now wherefore stoppest me?

'The Bridegroom's doors are open'd wide
    'And I am next of kin;
'The Guests are met, the Feast is set, –
    'May'st hear the merry din.

But still he holds the wedding-guest –
10   There was a Ship, quoth he –
'Nay, if thou'st got a laughsome tale,
    'Marinere! come with me.'

He holds him with his skinny hand,
    Quoth he, there was a Ship –
'Now get thee hence, thou grey-beard Loon!
    'Or my Staff shall make thee skip.

He holds him with his glittering eye –
    The wedding guest stood still
And listens like a three year's child;
20   The Marinere hath his will.

The wedding-guest sate on a stone,
    He cannot chuse but hear:
And thus spake on that ancyent man,
    The bright-eyed Marinere.

The Ship was cheer'd, the Harbour clear'd –
    Merrily did we drop
Below the Kirk, below the Hill,
    Below the Light-house top.

The Sun came up upon the left,
30   Out of the Sea came he:
And he shone bright, and on the right
    Went down into the Sea.

Higher and higher every day,
    Till over the mast at noon –
The wedding-guest here beat his breast,
    For he heard the loud bassoon.

The Bride hath pac'd into the Hall,
    Red as a rose is she;
Nodding their heads before her goes
40   The merry Minstralsy.

The wedding-guest he beat his breast,
    Yet he cannot chuse but hear:
And thus spake on that ancyent Man,
    The bright-eyed Marinere.

Listen, Stranger! Storm and Wind,
   A Wind and Tempest strong!
For days and weeks it play'd us freaks –
   Like Chaff we drove along.

Listen, Stranger! Mist and Snow,
50   And it grew wond'rous cauld:
And Ice mast-high came floating by
   As green as Emerauld.

And thro' the drifts the snowy clifts
   Did send a dismal sheen;
Ne shapes of men ne beasts we ken –
   The Ice was all between.

The Ice was here, the Ice was there,
   The Ice was all around:
It crack'd and growl'd, and roar'd and howl'd –
60   Like noises of a swound.

At length did cross an Albatross,
   Thorough the Fog it came;
And an it were a Christian Soul,
   We hail'd it in God's name.

The Marineres gave it biscuit-worms,
   And round and round it flew:
The Ice did split with a Thunder-fit;
   The Helmsman steer'd us thro'.

And a good south wind sprung up behind,
70   The Albatross did follow;
And every day for food or play
   Came to the Marinere's hollo!

In mist or cloud on mast or shroud
    It perch'd for vespers nine,
Whiles all the night thro' fog-smoke white
    Glimmer'd the white moon-shine.

'God save thee, ancyent Marinere!
    'From the fiends that plague thee thus –
'Why look'st thou so?' – with my cross bow
80   I shot the Albatross.

Part II

The Sun came up upon the right,
    Out of the Sea came he;
And broad as a weft upon the left
    Went down into the Sea.

And the good south wind still blew behind,
    But no sweet Bird did follow
Ne any day for food or play
    Came to the Marinere's hollo!

And I had done an hellish thing
90   And it would work 'em woe:
For all averr'd, I had kill'd the Bird
    That made the Breeze to blow.

Ne dim ne red, like God's own head,
    The glorious Sun uprist:
Then all averr'd, I had kill'd the Bird
    That brought the fog and mist.
'Twas right, said they, such birds to slay
    That bring the fog and mist.

The breezes blew, the white foam flew,
100   The furrow follow'd free:
We were the first that ever burst
    Into that silent Sea.

Down dropt the breeze, the Sails dropt down,
    'Twas sad as sad could be
And we did speak only to break
    The silence of the Sea.

All in a hot and copper sky
    The bloody sun at noon,
Right up above the mast did stand,
110   No bigger than the moon.

Day after day, day after day,
    We stuck, ne breath ne motion,
As idle as a painted Ship
    Upon a painted Ocean.

Water, water, every where
    And all the boards did shrink;
Water, water, every where
    Ne any drop to drink.

The very deeps did rot: O Christ!
120   That ever this should be!
Yea, slimy things did crawl with legs
    Upon the slimy Sea.

About, about, in reel and rout
    The Death-fires danc'd at night;
The water, like a witch's oils,
    Burnt green and blue and white.

And some in dreams assured were
   Of the Spirit that plagued us so:
Nine fathom deep he had follow'd us
130   From the Land of Mist and Snow.

And every tongue thro' utter drouth
   Was wither'd at the root;
We could not speak no more than if
   We had been choked with soot.

Ah wel-a-day! what evil looks
   Had I from old and young;
Instead of the Cross the Albatross
   About my neck was hung.

Part III

I saw a something in the Sky
140   No bigger than my fist;
At first it seem'd a little speck
   And then it seem'd a mist:
It mov'd and mov'd, and took at last
   A certain shape, I wist.

A speck, a mist, a shape, I wist!
   And still it ner'd and ner'd;
And, an it dodg'd a water-sprite,
   It plung'd and tack'd and veer'd.

With throat unslack'd, with black lips bak'd
150   Ne could we laugh, ne wail:
Then while thro' drouth all dumb they stood
I bit my arm and suck'd the blood
   And cry'd, A sail! a sail!

With throat unslack'd, with black lips bak'd
    Agape they hear'd me call:
Gramercy! they for joy did grin
And all at once their breath drew in
    As they were drinking all.

She doth not tack from side to side –
160   Hither to work us weal
Withouten wind, withouten tide
    She steddies with upright keel.

The western wave was all a flame,
    The day was well nigh done!
Almost upon the western wave
    Rested the broad bright Sun;
When that strange shape drove suddenly
    Betwixt us and the Sun.

And strait the Sun was fleck'd with bars
170   (Heaven's mother send us grace)
As if thro' a dungeon grate he peer'd
    With broad and burning face.

Alas! (thought I, and my heart beat loud)
    How fast she neres and neres!
Are those *her* Sails that glance in the Sun
    Like restless gossameres?

Are these *her* naked ribs, which fleck'd
    The sun that did behind them peer?
And are these two all, all the crew,
180   That woman and her fleshless Pheere?

His bones were black with many a crack,
    All black and bare, I ween;
Jet-black and bare, save where with rust
Of mouldy damps and charnel crust
    They're patch'd with purple and green.

Her lips are red, *her* looks are free,
    Her locks are yellow as gold:
Her skin is as white as leprosy,
And she is far liker Death than he;
190   Her flesh makes the still air cold.

The naked Hulk alongside came
    And the Twain were playing dice;
'The Game is done! I've won, I've won!'
    Quoth she, and whistled thrice.

A gust of wind sterte up behind
    And whistled thro' his bones;
Thro' the holes of his eyes and the hole of his mouth
    Half-whistles and half-groans.

With never a whisper in the Sea
200   Off darts the Spectre-ship;
While clombe above the Eastern bar
The horned Moon, with one bright Star
    Almost atween the tips.

One after one by the horned Moon
    (Listen, O Stranger! to me)
Each turn'd his face with a ghastly pang
    And curs'd me with his ee.

Four times fifty living men,
   With never a sigh or groan,
210 With heavy thump, a lifeless lump
   They dropp'd down one by one.

Their souls did from their bodies fly, –
   They fled to bliss or woe;
And every soul it pass'd me by,
   Like the whiz of my Cross-bow.

Part IV

'I fear thee, ancyent Marinere!
   'I fear thy skinny hand;
'And thou art long and lank and brown –
   'As is the ribb'd Sea-sand.

220 'I fear thee and thy glittering eye
   'And thy skinny hand so brown –
Fear not, fear not, thou wedding guest!
   This body dropt not down.

Alone, alone, all all alone
   Alone on the wide wide Sea;
And Christ would take no pity on
   My soul in agony.

The many men so beautiful,
   And they all dead did lie!
230 And a million million slimy things
   Liv'd on – and so did I.

I look'd upon the rotting Sea,
 And drew my eyes away;
I look'd upon the eldritch deck,
 And there the dead men lay.

I look'd to Heaven, and try'd to pray;
 But or ever a prayer had gusht,
A wicked whisper came and made
 My heart as dry as dust.

240 I clos'd my lids and kept them close,
 Till the balls like pulses beat;
For the sky and the sea, and the sea and the sky
Lay like a load on my weary eye,
 And the dead were at my feet.

The cold sweat melted from their limbs,
 Ne rot, ne reek did they;
The look with which they look'd on me,
 Had never pass'd away.

An orphan's curse would drag to Hell
250 A spirit from on high:
But O! more horrible than that
 Is the curse in a dead man's eye!
Seven days, seven nights I saw that curse,
 And yet I could not die.

The moving Moon went up the sky
 And no where did abide:
Softly she was going up
 And a star or two beside

Her beams bemock'd the sultry main
260 Like morning frosts yspread;
But where the ship's huge shadow lay,
The charmed water burnt alway
 A still and awful red.

Beyond the shadow of the ship
 I watch'd the water-snakes:
They mov'd in tracks of shining white;
And when they rear'd, the elfish light
 Fell off in hoary flakes.

Within the shadow of the ship
270 I watch'd their rich attire:
Blue, glossy green, and velvet black
They coil'd and swam; and every track
 Was a flash of golden fire.

O happy living things! no tongue
 Their beauty might declare:
A spring of love gusht from my heart,
 And I bless'd them unaware!
Sure my kind saint took pity on me,
 And I bless'd them unaware.

280 The self-same moment I could pray;
 And from my neck so free
The Albatross fell off, and sank
 Like lead into the sea.

Part V

O sleep, it is a gentle thing
   Belov'd from pole to pole!
To Mary-queen the praise be yeven
She sent the gentle sleep from heaven
   That slid into my soul.

The silly buckets on the deck
290   That had so long remain'd,
I dreamt that they were fill'd with dew
   And when I awoke it rain'd.

My lips were wet, my throat was cold,
   My garments all were dank;
Sure I had drunken in my dreams
   And still my body drank.

I mov'd and could not feel my limbs,
   I was so light, almost
I thought that I had died in sleep,
300   And was a blessed Ghost.

The roaring wind! it roar'd far off,
   It did not come anear;
But with its sound it shook the sails
   That were so thin and sere.

The upper air bursts into life,
   And a hundred fire-flags sheen
To and fro they are hurried about;
And to and fro, and in and out
   The stars dance on between.

310 The coming wind doth roar more loud;
    The sails do sigh, like sedge:
The rain pours down from one black cloud
    And the Moon is at its edge.

Hark! hark! the thick black cloud is cleft,
    And the Moon is at its side:
Like waters shot from some high crag,
The lightning falls with never a jag
    A river steep and wide.

The strong wind reach'd the ship: it roar'd
320   And dropp'd down, like a stone!
Beneath the lightning and the moon
    The dead men gave a groan.

They groan'd, they stirr'd, they all uprose,
    Ne spake, ne mov'd their eyes:
It had been strange, even in a dream
    To have seen those dead men rise.

The helmsman steerd, the ship mov'd on;
    Yet never a breeze up-blew;
The Marineres all 'gan work the ropes,
330   Where they were wont to do:
They rais'd their limbs like lifeless tools –
    We were a ghastly crew.

The body of my brother's son
    Stood by me knee to knee:
The body and I pull'd at one rope,
    But he said nought to me –
And I quak'd to think of my own voice
    How frightful it would be!

The day-light dawn'd – they dropp'd their arms,
340   And cluster'd round the mast:
Sweet sounds rose slowly thro' their mouths
   And from their bodies pass'd.

Around, around, flew each sweet sound,
   Then darted to the sun:
Slowly the sounds came back again
   Now mix'd, now one by one.

Sometimes a dropping from the sky
   I heard the Lavrock sing;
Sometimes all little birds that are
350   How they seem'd to fill the sea and air
   With their sweet jargoning,

And now 'twas like all instruments,
   Now like a lonely flute;
And now it is an angel's song
   That makes the heavens be mute.

It ceas'd: yet still the sails made on
   A pleasant noise till noon,
A noise like of a hidden brook
   In the leafy month of June,
360   That to the sleeping woods all night
   Singeth a quiet tune.

Listen, O listen, thou Wedding-guest!
   'Marinere! thou hast thy will:
'For that, which comes out of thine eye, doth make
   'My body and soul to be still.'

Never sadder tale was told
   To a man of woman born:
Sadder and wiser thou wedding-guest!
   Thou'lt rise to morrow morn.

370 Never sadder tale was heard
   By a man of woman born:
The Marineres all return'd to work
   As silent as beforne.

The Marineres all 'gan pull the ropes,
   But look at me they n'old:
Thought I, I am as thin as air –
   They cannot me behold.

Till noon we silently sail'd on
   Yet never a breeze did breathe:
380 Slowly and smoothly went the ship
   Mov'd onward from beneath.

Under the keel nine fathom deep
   From the land of mist and snow
The spirit slid: and it was He
   That made the Ship to go.
The sails at noon left off their tune
   And the Ship stood still also.

The sun right up above the mast
   Had fix'd her to the ocean:
390 But in a minute she 'gan stir
   With a short uneasy motion –
Backwards and forwards half her length
   With a short uneasy motion.

Then, like a pawing horse let go,
    She made a sudden bound:
It flung the blood into my head,
    And I fell into a swound.

How long in that same fit I lay,
    I have not to declare;
400 But ere my living life return'd,
I heard and in my soul discern'd
    Two voices in the air,

'Is it he?' quoth one, 'Is this the man?
    'By him who died on cross,
'With his cruel bow he lay'd full low
    'The harmless Albatross.

'The spirit who 'bideth by himself
    'In the land of mist and snow,
'He lov'd the bird that lov'd the man
410   'Who shot him with his bow.

The other was a softer voice,
    As soft as honey-dew:
Quoth he the man hath penance done,
    And penance more will do.

Part VI

FIRST VOICE
'But tell me, tell me! speak again,
    'Thy soft response renewing –
'What makes that ship drive on so fast?
    'What is the Ocean doing?

SECOND VOICE
'Still as a Slave before his Lord,
420   'The Ocean hath no blast:
'His great bright eye most silently
    'Up to the moon is cast –

'If he may know which way to go,
    'For she guides him smooth or grim.
'See, brother, see! how graciously
    'She looketh down on him.

FIRST VOICE
'But why drives on that ship so fast
    'Withouten wave or wind?

SECOND VOICE
'The air is cut away before,
430   'And closes from behind.

'Fly, brother, fly!' more high, more high,
    'Or we shall be belated:
'For slow and slow that ship will go,
    'When the Marinere's trance is abated.'

I woke, and we were sailing on
    As in a gentle weather:
'Twas night, calm night, the moon was high;
    The dead men stood together.

All stood together on the deck,
440   For a charnel-dungeon fitter:
All fix'd on me their stony eyes
    That in the moon did glitter.

The pang, the curse, with which they died,
    Had never pass'd away:
I could not draw my een from theirs
    Ne turn them up to pray.

And in its time the spell was snapt,
    And I could move my een:
I look'd far-forth, but little saw
450   Of what might else be seen.

Like one, that on a lonely road
    Doth walk in fear and dread,
And having once turn'd round, walks on
    And turns no more his head:
Because he knows, a frightful fiend
    Doth close behind him tread.

But soon there breath'd a wind on me,
    Ne sound ne motion made:
Its path was not upon the sea
460   In ripple or in shade.

It rais'd my hair, it fann'd my cheek,
    Like a meadow-gale of spring –
It mingled strangely with my fears,
    Yet it felt like a welcoming.

Swiftly, swiftly flew the ship,
    Yet she sail'd softly too:
Sweetly, sweetly blew the breeze –
    On me alone it blew.

O dream of joy! is this indeed
470   The light-house top I see?
Is this the Hill? Is this the Kirk?
    Is this mine own countrée?

We drifted o'er the Harbour-bar,
  And I with sobs did pray –
'O let me be awake, my God!
  'Or let me sleep alway!'

The harbour-bay was clear as glass,
  So smoothly it was strewn!
And on the bay the moon light lay,
480 And the shadow of the moon.

The moonlight bay was white all o'er,
  Till rising from the same,
Full many shapes, that shadows were,
  Like as of torches came.

A little distance from the prow
  Those dark-red shadows were;
But soon I saw that my own flesh
  Was red as in a glare.

I turn'd my head in fear and dread,
490 And by the holy rood,
The bodies had advanc'd, and now
  Before the mast they stood.

They lifted up their stiff right arms,
  They held them strait and tight;
And each right-arm burnt like a torch,
  A torch that's borne upright.
Their stony eye-balls glitter'd on
  In the red and smoky light.

I pray'd and turn'd my head away
500 Forth looking as before.
There was no breeze upon the bay,
  No wave against the shore.

The rock shone bright, the kirk no less
  That stands above the rock:
The moonlight steep'd in silentness
  The steady weathercock.

And the bay was white with silent light,
  Till rising from the same
Full many shapes, that shadows were,
510 In crimson colours came.

A little distance from the prow
  Those crimson shadows were:
I turn'd my eyes upon the deck –
  O Christ! what saw I there?

Each corse lay flat, lifeless and flat;
  And by the Holy rood
A man all light, a seraph-man,
  On every corse there stood.

This seraph-band, each wav'd his hand:
520 It was a heavenly sight:
They stood as signals to the land,
  Each one a lovely light:

This seraph-band, each wav'd his hand,
  No voice did they impart –
No voice; but O! the silence sank,
  Like music on my heart.

Eftsones I heard the dash of oars,
   I heard the pilot's cheer:
My head was turn'd perforce away
530   And I saw a boat appear.

Then vanish'd all the lovely lights;
   The bodies rose anew:
With silent pace, each to his place,
   Came back the ghastly crew.
The wind, that shade nor motion made,
   On me alone it blew.

The pilot, and the pilot's boy
   I heard them coming fast:
Dear Lord in Heaven! it was a joy,
540   The dead men could not blast.

I saw a third – I heard his voice:
   It is the Hermit good!
He singeth loud his godly hymns
   That he makes in the wood.
He'll shrieve my soul, he'll wash away
   The Albatross's blood.

Part VII

This Hermit good lives in that wood
   Which slopes down to the Sea.
How loudly his sweet voice he rears!
550 He loves to talk with Marineres
   That come from a far Contrée.

He kneels at morn and noon and eve –
   He hath a cushion plump:
It is the moss, that wholly hides
   The rotted old Oak-stump.

The Skiff-boat ne'rd: I heard them talk,
  'Why, this is strange, I trow!
'Where are those lights so many and fair
  'That signal made but now?

560 'Strange, by my faith! the Hermit said –
  'And they answer'd not our cheer.
'The planks look warp'd, and see those sails
  'How thin they are and sere!
'I never saw aught like to them
  'Unless perchance it were

'The skeletons of leaves that lag
  'My forest brook along:
'When the Ivy-tod is heavy with snow,
'And the Owlet whoops to the wolf below
570 'That eats the she-wolf's young.

'Dear Lord! it has a fiendish look –
  (The Pilot made reply)
'I am a-fear'd. – 'Push on, push on!
  'Said the Hermit cheerily.

The Boat came closer to the Ship,
  But I ne spake ne stirr'd!
The Boat came close beneath the Ship,
  And strait a sound was heard!

Under the water it rumbled on,
580 Still louder and more dread:
It reach'd the Ship, it split the bay;
  The Ship went down like lead.

Stunn'd by that loud and dreadful sound,
    Which sky and ocean smote:
Like one that hath been seven days drown'd
    My body lay afloat:
But, swift as dreams, myself I found
    Within the Pilot's boat.

Upon the whirl, where sank the Ship,
590   The boat spun round and round:
And all was still, save that the hill
    Was telling of the sound.

I mov'd my lips: the Pilot shriek'd
    And fell down in a fit.
The Holy Hermit rais'd his eyes
    And pray'd where he did sit.

I took the oars: the Pilot's boy,
    Who now doth crazy go,
Laugh'd loud and long, and all the while
600   His eyes went to and fro,
'Ha! ha!' quoth he – 'full plain I see,
    'The devil knows how to row.'

And now all in mine own Countrée
    I stood on the firm land!
The Hermit stepp'd forth from the boat,
    And scarcely he could stand.

'O shrieve me, shrieve me, holy Man!
    The Hermit cross'd his brow –
'Say quick,' quoth he, 'I bid thee say
610   'What manner man art thou?

Forthwith this frame of mine was wrench'd
   With a woeful agony,
Which forc'd me to begin my tale
   And then it left me free.

Since then at an uncertain hour,
   Now oftimes and now fewer,
That anguish comes and makes me tell
   My ghastly aventure.

I pass, like night, from land to land;
620   I have strange power of speech;
The moment that his face I see
I know the man that must hear me;
   To him my tale I teach.

What loud uproar bursts from that door!
   The Wedding-guests are there;
But in the Garden-bower the Bride
   And Bride-maids singing are:
And hark the little Vesper-bell
   Which biddeth me to prayer.

630 O Wedding-guest! this soul hath been
   Alone on a wide wide sea:
So lonely 'twas, that God himself
   Scarce seemed there to be.

O sweeter than the Marriage-feast,
   'Tis sweeter far to me
To walk together to the Kirk
   With a goodly company.

To walk together to the Kirk
    And all together pray,
640 While each to his great father bends,
Old men, and babes, and loving friends,
    And Youths, and Maidens gay.

Farewell, farewell! but this I tell
    To thee, thou wedding-guest!
He prayeth well who loveth well
    Both man and bird and beast.

He prayeth best who loveth best,
    All things both great and small:
For the dear God, who loveth us,
650   He made and loveth all.

The Marinere, whose eye is bright,
    Whose beard with age is hoar,
Is gone; and now the wedding-guest
    Turn'd from the bridegroom's door.

He went, like one that hath been stunn'd
    And is of sense forlorn:
A sadder and a wiser man
    He rose the morrow morn.

The Foster-Mother's Tale

A dramatic fragment

FOSTER-MOTHER
I never saw the man whom you describe.

MARIA
'Tis strange! he spake of you familiarly
As mine and Albert's common Foster-mother.

FOSTER-MOTHER
Now blessings on the man, whoe'er he be,
That joined your names with mine! O my sweet lady,
As often as I think of those dear times
When you two little ones would stand at eve
On each side of my chair, and make me learn
All you had learnt in the day; and how to talk
10   In gentle phrase, then bid me sing to you –
'Tis more like heaven to come than what *has* been.

MARIA
O my dear Mother! this strange man has left me
Troubled with wilder fancies, than the moon
Breeds in the love-sick maid who gazes at it,
Till lost in inward vision, with wet eye
She gazes idly! – But that entrance, Mother!

FOSTER-MOTHER
Can no one hear? It is a perilous tale!

MARIA
No one.

FOSTER-MOTHER
　　　　My husband's father told it me,
Poor old Leoni! – Angels rest his soul!
20　He was a woodman, and could fell and saw
With lusty arm. You know that huge round beam
Which props the hanging wall of the old chapel?
Beneath that tree, while yet it was a tree
He found a baby wrapt in mosses, lined
With thistle-beards, and such small locks of wool
As hang on brambles. Well, he brought him home,
And reared him at the then Lord Velez' cost.
And so the babe grew up a pretty boy,
A pretty boy, but most unteachable –
30　And never learnt a prayer, nor told a bead,
But knew the names of birds, and mocked their notes,
And whistled, as he were a bird himself:
And all the autumn 'twas his only play
To get the seeds of wild flowers, and to plant them
With earth and water, on the stumps of trees.
A Friar, who gathered simples in the wood,
A grey-haired man – he loved this little boy,
The boy loved him – and, when the Friar taught him,
He soon could write with the pen: and from that time,
40　Lived chiefly at the Convent or the Castle.
So he became a very learned youth.
But Oh! poor wretch! – he read, and read, and read,
'Till his brain turned – and ere his twentieth year,
He had unlawful thoughts of many things:
And though he prayed, he never loved to pray
With holy men, nor in a holy place –
But yet his speech, it was so soft and sweet,
The late Lord Velez ne'er was wearied with him.
And once, as by the north side of the Chapel
50　They stood together, chained in deep discourse,

The earth heaved under them with such a groan,
That the wall tottered, and had well-nigh fallen
Right on their heads. My Lord was sorely frightened;
A fever seized him, and he made confession
Of all the heretical and lawless talk
Which brought this judgment: so the youth was seized
And cast into that hole. My husband's father
Sobbed like a child – it almost broke his heart:
And once as he was working in the cellar,
60 He heard a voice distinctly; 'twas the youth's,
Who sung a doleful song about green fields,
How sweet it were on lake or wild savannah,
To hunt for food, and be a naked man,
And wander up and down at liberty.
He always doted on the youth, and now
His love grew desperate; and defying death,
He made that cunning entrance I described:
And the young man escaped.

MARIA
         'Tis a sweet tale:
Such as would lull a listening child to sleep,
70 His rosy face besoiled with unwiped tears. –
And what became of him?

FOSTER-MOTHER
         He went on ship-board
With those bold voyagers, who made discovery
Of golden lands. Leoni's younger brother
Went likewise, and when he returned to Spain,
He told Leoni, that the poor mad youth,
Soon after they arrived in that new world,
In spite of his dissuasion, seized a boat,
And all alone, set sail by silent moonlight

Up a great river, great as any sea,
80 And ne'er was heard of more: but 'tis supposed,
He lived and died among the savage men.

Lines left upon a Seat in a Yew-tree

WHICH STANDS NEAR THE LAKE OF ESTHWAITE,
ON A DESOLATE PART OF THE SHORE,
YET COMMANDING A BEAUTIFUL PROSPECT

– Nay, Traveller! rest. This lonely yew-tree stands
Far from all human dwelling: what if here
No sparkling rivulet spread the verdant herb;
What if these barren boughs the bee not loves;
Yet, if the wind breathe soft, the curling waves,
That break against the shore, shall lull thy mind
By one soft impulse saved from vacancy.
——————————Who he was
That piled these stones, and with the mossy sod
10 First covered o'er, and taught this aged tree,
Now wild, to bend its arms in circling shade,
I well remember. – He was one who own'd
No common soul. In youth, by genius nurs'd,
And big with lofty views, he to the world
Went forth, pure in his heart, against the taint
Of dissolute tongues, 'gainst jealousy, and hate,
And scorn, against all enemies prepared,
All but neglect: and so, his spirit damped
At once, with rash disdain he turned away,
20 And with the food of pride sustained his soul
In solitude. – Stranger! these gloomy boughs

43

Had charms for him; and here he loved to sit,
His only visitants a straggling sheep,
The stone-chat, or the glancing sand-piper;
And on these barren rocks, with juniper,
And heath, and thistle, thinly sprinkled o'er,
Fixing his downward eye, he many an hour
A morbid pleasure nourished, tracing here
An emblem of his own unfruitful life:
30 And lifting up his head, he then would gaze
On the more distant scene; how lovely 'tis
Thou seest, and he would gaze till it became
Far lovelier, and his heart could not sustain
The beauty still more beauteous. Nor, that time,
Would he forget those beings, to whose minds,
Warm from the labours of benevolence,
The world, and man himself, appeared a scene
Of kindred loveliness: then he would sigh
With mournful joy, to think that others felt
40 What he must never feel: and so, lost man!
On visionary views would fancy feed,
Till his eye streamed with tears. In this deep vale
He died, this seat his only monument.

If thou be one whose heart the holy forms
Of young imagination have kept pure,
Stranger! henceforth be warned; and know, that pride,
Howe'er disguised in its own majesty,
Is littleness; that he, who feels contempt
For any living thing, hath faculties
50 Which he has never used; that thought with him
Is in its infancy. The man, whose eye
Is ever on himself, doth look on one,
The least of nature's works, one who might move
The wise man to that scorn which wisdom holds

Unlawful, ever. O, be wiser thou!
Instructed that true knowledge leads to love,
True dignity abides with him alone
Who, in the silent hour of inward thought,
Can still suspect, and still revere himself,
60   In lowliness of heart.

The Nightingale

A CONVERSATIONAL POEM, WRITTEN IN APRIL, 1798

No cloud, no relique of the sunken day
Distinguishes the West, no long thin slip
Of sullen Light, no obscure trembling hues.
Come, we will rest on this old mossy Bridge!
You see the glimmer of the stream beneath.
But hear no murmuring: it flows silently
O'er its soft bed of verdure. All is still,
A balmy night! and tho' the stars be dim,
Yet let us think upon the vernal showers
10   That gladden the green earth, and we shall find
A pleasure in the dimness of the stars.
And hark! the Nightingale begins its song,
'Most musical, most melancholy'* Bird!

---

* *'Most musical, most melancholy'*. This passage in Milton possesses an excellence
far superior to that of mere description: it is spoken in the character of the
melancholy Man, and has therefore a *dramatic* property. The Author makes this
remark, to rescue himself from the charge of having alluded with levity to a line
in Milton: a charge than which none could be more painful to him, except
perhaps that of having ridiculed his Bible.

45

A melancholy Bird? O idle thought!
In nature there is nothing melancholy.
– But some night-wandering Man, whose heart was
      pierc'd
With the remembrance of a grievous wrong,
Or slow distemper or neglected love,
(And so, poor Wretch! fill'd all things with himself
20   And made all gentle sounds tell back the tale
Of his own sorrows) he and such as he
First nam'd these notes a melancholy strain;
And many a poet echoes the conceit,
Poet, who hath been building up the rhyme
When he had better far have stretch'd his limbs
Beside a brook in mossy forest-dell
By sun or moonlight, to the influxes
Of shapes and sounds and shifting elements
Surrendering his whole spirit, of his song
30   And of his fame forgetful! so his fame
Should share in nature's immortality,
A venerable thing! and so his song
Should make all nature lovelier, and itself
Be lov'd, like nature! – But 'twill not be so;
And youths and maidens most poetical
Who lose the deep'ning twilights of the spring
In ball-rooms and hot theatres, they still
Full of meek sympathy must heave their sighs
O'er Philomela's pity-pleading strains.
40   My Friend, and my Friend's Sister! we have learnt
A different lore: we may not thus profane
Nature's sweet voices always full of love
And joyance! 'Tis the merry Nightingale
That crowds, and hurries, and precipitates
With fast thick warble his delicious notes,
As he were fearful, that an April night

Would be too short for him to utter forth
His love-chant, and disburthen his full soul
Of all its music! And I know a grove
50 Of large extent, hard by a castle huge
Which the great lord inhabits not: and so
This grove is wild with tangling underwood,
And the trim walks are broken up, and grass,
Thin grass and king-cups grow within the paths.
But never elsewhere in one place I knew
So many Nightingales: and far and near
In wood and thicket over the wide grove
They answer and provoke each other's songs –
With skirmish and capricious passagings,
60 And murmurs musical and swift jug jug
And one low piping sound more sweet than all –
Stirring the air with such an harmony,
That should you close your eyes, you might almost
Forget it was not day! On moonlight bushes,
Whose dewy leafits are but half disclos'd,
You may perchance behold them on the twigs,
Their bright, bright eyes, their eyes both bright
        and full,
Glistning, while many a glow-worm in the shade
Lights up her love-torch.

                        A most gentle maid
70 Who dwelleth in her hospitable home
Hard by the Castle, and at latest eve,
(Even like a Lady vow'd and dedicate
To something more than nature in the grove)
Glides thro' the pathways; she knows all their notes,
That gentle Maid! and oft, a moment's space,
What time the moon was lost behind a cloud,
Hath heard a pause of silence: till the Moon

Emerging, hath awaken'd earth and sky
With one sensation, and those wakeful Birds
80 Have all burst forth in choral minstrelsy,
As if one quick and sudden Gale had swept
An hundred airy harps! And she hath watch'd
Many a Nightingale perch giddily
On blosmy twig still swinging from the breeze,
And to that motion tune his wanton song,
Like tipsy Joy that reels with tossing head.

Farewell, O Warbler! till to-morrow eve,
And you, my friends! farewell, a short farewell!
We have been loitering long and pleasantly,
90 And now for our dear homes. – That strain again!
Full fain it would delay me! – My dear Babe,
Who, capable of no articulate sound,
Mars all things with his imitative lisp,
How he would place his hand beside his ear,
His little hand, the small forefinger up,
And bid us listen! And I deem it wise
To make him Nature's playmate. He knows well
The evening star: and once when he awoke
In most distressful mood (some inward pain
100 Had made up that strange thing, an infant's dream)
I hurried with him to our orchard plot,
And he beholds the moon, and hush'd at once
Suspends his sobs, and laughs most silently,
While his fair eyes that swam with undropt tears
Did glitter in the yellow moon-beam! Well –
It is a father's tale. But if that Heaven
Should give me life, his childhood shall grow up
Familiar with these songs, that with the night
He may associate Joy! Once more farewell,
110 Sweet Nightingale! once more, my friends! farewell.

The Female Vagrant

By Derwent's side my Father's cottage stood,
(The Woman thus her artless story told)
One field, a flock, and what the neighbouring flood
Supplied, to him were more than mines of gold.
Light was my sleep; my days in transport roll'd:
With thoughtless joy I stretch'd along the shore
My father's nets, or watched, when from the fold
High o'er the cliffs I led my fleecy store,
A dizzy depth below! his boat and twinkling oar.

10 My father was a good and pious man,
An honest man by honest parents bred,
And I believe that, soon as I began
To lisp, he made me kneel beside my bed,
And in his hearing there my prayers I said:
And afterwards, by my good father taught,
I read, and loved the books in which I read;
For books in every neighbouring house I sought,
And nothing to my mind a sweeter pleasure brought.

Can I forget what charms did once adorn
20 My garden, stored with pease, and mint, and thyme,
And rose and lilly for the sabbath morn?
The sabbath bells, and their delightful chime;
The gambols and wild freaks at shearing time;
My hens's rich nest through long grass scarce espied;
The cowslip-gathering at May's dewy prime;
The swans, that, when I sought the water-side,
From far to meet me came, spreading their snowy
     pride.

The staff I yet remember which upbore
The bending body of my active sire;
30   His seat beneath the honeyed sycamore
When the bees hummed, and chair by winter fire;
When market-morning came, the neat attire
With which, though bent on haste, myself I deck'd;
My watchful dog, whose starts of furious ire,
When stranger passed, so often I have check'd;
The red-breast known for years, which at my
      casement peck'd.

The suns of twenty summers danced along, –
Ah! little marked, how fast they rolled away:
Then rose a mansion proud our woods among,
40   And cottage after cottage owned its sway,
No joy to see a neighbouring house, or stray
Through pastures not his own, the master took;
My Father dared his greedy wish gainsay;
He loved his old hereditary nook,
And ill could I the thought of such sad parting brook.

But, when he had refused the proffered gold,
To cruel injuries he became a prey,
Sore-traversed in whate'er he bought and sold:
His troubles grew upon him day by day,
50   Till all his substance fell into decay.
His little range of water was denied;*
All but the bed where his old body lay,
All, all was seized, and weeping, side by side,
We sought a home where we uninjured might abide.

---

* Several of the Lakes in the north of England are let out to different Fishermen, in parcels marked out by imaginary lines drawn from rock to rock.

Can I forget that miserable hour,
When from the last hill-top, my sire surveyed,
Peering above the trees, the steeple tower,
That on his marriage-day sweet music made?
Till then he hoped his bones might there be laid,
60   Close by my mother in their native bowers:
Bidding me trust in God, he stood and prayed, –
I could not pray: – through tears that fell in showers,
Glimmer'd our dear-loved home, alas! no longer ours!

There was a youth whom I had loved so long,
That when I loved him not I cannot say.
'Mid the green mountains many and many a song
We two had sung, like little birds in May.
When we began to tire of childish play
We seemed still more and more to prize each other:
70   We talked of marriage and our marriage day;
And I in truth did love him like a brother,
For never could I hope to meet with such another.

His father said, that to a distant town
He must repair, to ply the artist's trade.
What tears of bitter grief till then unknown!
What tender vows our last sad kiss delayed!
To him we turned: – we had no other aid.
Like one revived, upon his neck I wept,
And her whom he had loved in joy, he said
80   He well could love in grief: his faith he kept;
And in a quiet home once more my father slept.

Four years each day with daily bread was blest,
By constant toil and constant prayer supplied.
Three lovely infants lay upon my breast;
And often, viewing their sweet smiles, I sighed,
And knew not why. My happy father died
When sad distress reduced the children's meal:
Thrice happy! that from him the grave did hide
The empty loom, cold hearth, and silent wheel,
90   And tears that flowed for ills which patience
        could not heal.

'Twas a hard change, an evil time was come;
We had no hope, and no relief could gain.
But soon, with proud parade, the noisy drum
Beat round, to sweep the streets of want and pain.
My husband's arms now only served to strain
Me and his children hungering in his view:
In such dismay my prayers and tears were vain:
To join those miserable men he flew;
And now to the sea-coast, with numbers more,
    we drew.

100   There foul neglect for months and months we bore,
Nor yet the crowded fleet its anchor stirred.
Green fields before us and our native shore,
By fever, from polluted air incurred,
Ravage was made, for which no knell was heard.
Fondly we wished, and wished away, nor knew,
'Mid that long sickness, and those hopes deferr'd,
That happier days we never more must view:
The parting signal streamed, at last the land withdrew,

But from delay the summer calms were past.
110 On as we drove, the equinoctial deep
Ran mountains-high before the howling blast.
We gazed with terror on the gloomy sleep
Of them that perished in the whirlwind's sweep,
Untaught that soon such anguish must ensue,
Our hopes such harvest of affliction reap,
That we the mercy of the waves should rue.
We reached the western world, a poor, devoted crew.

Oh! dreadful price of being to resign
All that is dear *in* being! better far
120 In Want's most lonely cave till death to pine,
Unseen, unheard, unwatched by any star;
Or in the streets and walks where proud men are,
Better our dying bodies to obtrude,
Than dog-like, wading at the heels of war,
Protract a curst existence, with the brood
That lap (their very nourishment!) their brother's
blood.

The pains and plagues that on our heads came down,
Disease and famine, agony and fear,
In wood or wilderness, in camp or town,
130 It would thy brain unsettle even to hear.
All perished – all, in one remorseless year,
Husband and children! one by one, by sword
And ravenous plague, all perished: every tear
Dried up, despairing, desolate, on board
A British ship I waked, as from a trance restored.

Peaceful as some immeasurable plain
By the first beams of dawning light impress'd,
In the calm sunshine slept the glittering main.
The very ocean has its hour of rest,
140 That comes not to the human mourner's breast.
Remote from man, and storms of mortal care,
A heavenly silence did the waves invest;
I looked and looked along the silent air,
Until it seemed to bring a joy to my despair.

Ah! how unlike those late terrific sleeps!
And groans, that rage of racking famine spoke,
Where looks inhuman dwelt on festering heaps!
The breathing pestilence that rose like smoke!
The shriek that from the distant battle broke!
150 The mine's dire earthquake, and the pallid host
Driven by the bomb's incessant thunder-stroke
To loathsome vaults, where heart-sick anguish toss'd,
Hope died, and fear itself in agony was lost!

Yet does that burst of woe congeal my frame,
When the dark streets appeared to heave and gape,
While like a sea the storming army came,
And Fire from Hell reared his gigantic shape,
And Murder, by the ghastly gleam, and Rape
Seized their joint prey, the mother and the child!
160 But from these crazing thoughts my brain, escape!
– For weeks the balmy air breathed soft and mild,
And on the gliding vessel Heaven and Ocean smiled.

Some mighty gulph of separation past,
I seemed transported to another world: –
A thought resigned with pain, when from the mast
The impatient mariner the sail unfurl'd,
And whistling, called the wind that hardly curled
The silent sea. From the sweet thoughts of home,
And from all hope I was forever hurled.
For me – farthest from earthly port to roam
Was best, could I but shun the spot where man
        might come.

And oft, robb'd of my perfect mind, I thought
At last my feet a resting-place had found:
Here will I weep in peace, (so fancy wrought,)
Roaming the illimitable waters round;
Here watch, of every human friend disowned,
All day, my ready tomb the ocean-flood –
To break my dream the vessel reached its bound:
And homeless near a thousand homes I stood,
And near a thousand tables pined, and wanted food.

By grief enfeebled was I turned adrift,
Helpless as sailor cast on desart rock;
Nor morsel to my mouth that day did lift,
Nor dared my hand at any door to knock.
I lay, where with his drowsy mates, the cock
From the cross timber of an out-house hung;
How dismal tolled, that night, the city clock!
At morn my sick heart hunger scarcely stung,
Nor to the beggar's language could I frame my tongue.

170

180

55

190   So passed another day, and so the third:
Then did I try, in vain, the crowd's resort,
In deep despair by frightful wishes stirr'd,
Near the sea-side I reached a ruined fort:
There, pains which nature could no more support,
With blindness linked, did on my vitals fall;
Dizzy my brain, with interruption short
Of hideous sense; I sunk, nor step could crawl,
And thence was borne away to neighbouring hospital.

Recovery came with food: but still, my brain
200   Was weak, nor of the past had memory.
I heard my neighbours, in their beds, complain
Of many things which never troubled me;
Of feet still bustling round with busy glee,
Of looks where common kindness had no part,
Of service done with careless cruelty,
Fretting the fever round the languid heart,
And groans, which, as they said, would make a
    dead man start.

These things just served to stir the torpid sense,
Nor pain nor pity in my bosom raised.
210   Memory, though slow, returned with strength;
    and thence
Dismissed, again on open day I gazed,
At houses, men, and common light, amazed.
The lanes I sought, and as the sun retired,
Came, where beneath the trees a faggot blazed;
The wild brood saw me weep, my fate enquired,
And gave me food, and rest, more welcome, more
    desired.

My heart is touched to think that men like these,
The rude earth's tenants, were my first relief:
How kindly did they paint their vagrant ease!
220 And their long holiday that feared not grief,
For all belonged to all, and each was chief.
No plough their sinews strained; on grating road
No wain they drove, and yet, the yellow sheaf
In every vale for their delight was stowed:
For them, in nature's meads, the milky udder flowed.

Semblance, with straw and panniered ass, they made
Of potters wandering on from door to door:
But life of happier sort to me pourtrayed,
And other joys my fancy to allure;
230 The bag-pipe dinning on the midnight moor
In barn uplighted, and companions boon
Well met from far with revelry secure,
In depth of forest glade, when jocund June
Rolled fast along the sky his warm and genial moon.

But ill it suited me, in journey dark
O'er moor and mountain, midnight theft to hatch;
To charm the surly house-dog's faithful bark,
Or hang on tiptoe at the lifted latch;
The gloomy lantern, and the dim blue match,
240 The black disguise, the warning whistle shrill,
And ear still busy on its nightly watch,
 Were not for me, brought up in nothing ill;
Besides, on griefs so fresh my thoughts were
    brooding still.

What could I do, unaided and unblest?
Poor Father! gone was every friend of thine:
And kindred of dead husband are at best
Small help, and, after marriage such as mine,
With little kindness would to me incline.
Ill was I then for toil or service fit:
250 With tears whose course no effort could confine,
By high-way side forgetful would I sit
Whole hours, my idle arms in moping sorrow knit.

I lived upon the mercy of the fields,
And oft of cruelty the sky accused;
On hazard, or what general bounty yields,
Now coldly given, now utterly refused.
The fields I for my bed have often used:
But, what afflicts my peace with keenest ruth
Is, that I have my inner self abused,
260 Foregone the home delight of constant truth,
And clear and open soul, so prized in fearless youth.

Three years a wanderer, often have I view'd,
In tears, the sun towards that country tend
Where my poor heart lost all its fortitude:
And now across this moor my steps I bend –
Oh! tell me whither – for no earthly friend
Have I. – She ceased, and weeping turned away,
As if because her tale was at an end
She wept; – because she had no more to say
270 Of that perpetual weight which on her spirit lay.

Goody Blake and Harry Gill

A TRUE STORY

Oh! what's the matter? what's the matter?
What is't that ails young Harry Gill?
That evermore his teeth they chatter,
Chatter, chatter, chatter still.
Of waistcoats Harry has no lack,
Good duffle grey, and flannel fine;
He has a blanket on his back,
And coats enough to smother nine.

In March, December, and in July,
10 'Tis all the same with Harry Gill;
The neighbours tell, and tell you truly,
His teeth they chatter, chatter still.
At night, at morning, and at noon,
'Tis all the same with Harry Gill;
Beneath the sun, beneath the moon,
His teeth they chatter, chatter still.

Young Harry was a lusty drover,
And who so stout of limb as he?
His cheeks were red as ruddy clover,
20 His voice was like the voice of three.
Auld Goody Blake was old and poor,
Ill fed she was, and thinly clad;
And any man who pass'd her door,
Might see how poor a hut she had.

All day she spun in her poor dwelling,
And then her three hours' work at night!
Alas! 'twas hardly worth the telling,
It would not pay for candle-light.
– This woman dwelt in Dorsetshire,
30 Her hut was on a cold hill-side,
And in that country coals are dear,
For they come far by wind and tide.

By the same fire to boil their pottage,
Two poor old dames, as I have known,
Will often live in one small cottage,
But she, poor woman, dwelt alone.
'Twas well enough when summer came,
The long, warm, lightsome summer-day,
Then at her door the *canty* dame
40 Would sit, as any linnet gay.

But when the ice our streams did fetter,
Oh! then how her old bones would shake!
You would have said, if you had met her,
'Twas a hard time for Goody Blake.
Her evenings then were dull and dead;
Sad case it was, as you may think,
For very cold to go to bed,
And then for cold not sleep a wink.

Oh joy for her! when e'er in winter
50 The winds at night had made a rout,
And scatter'd many a lusty splinter,
And many a rotten bough about.
Yet never had she, well or sick,
As every man who knew her says,
A pile before-hand, wood or stick,
Enough to warm her for three days.

60

Now, when the frost was past enduring,
And made her poor old bones to ache,
Could any thing be more alluring,
60 Than an old hedge to Goody Blake?
And now and then, it must be said,
When her old bones were cold and chill,
She left her fire, or left her bed,
To seek the hedge of Harry Gill.

Now Harry he had long suspected
This trespass of old Goody Blake,
And vow'd that she should be detected,
And he on her would vengeance take.
And oft from his warm fire he'd go,
70 And to the fields his road would take,
And there, at night, in frost and snow,
He watch'd to seize old Goody Blake.

And once, behind a rick of barley,
Thus looking out did Harry stand;
The moon was full and shining clearly,
And crisp with frost the stubble-land.
– He hears a noise – he's all awake –
Again? – on tip-toe down the hill
He softly creeps – 'Tis Goody Blake,
80 She's at the hedge of Harry Gill.

Right glad was he when he beheld her:
Stick after stick did Goody pull,
He stood behind a bush of elder,
Till she had filled her apron full.
When with her load she turned about,
The bye-road back again to take,
He started forward with a shout,
And sprang upon poor Goody Blake.

And fiercely by the arm he took her,
90   And by the arm he held her fast,
And fiercely by the arm he shook her,
And cried, 'I've caught you then at last!'
Then Goody, who had nothing said,
Her bundle from her lap let fall;
And kneeling on the sticks, she pray'd
To God that is the judge of all.

She pray'd, her wither'd hand uprearing,
While Harry held her by the arm –
'God! who art never out of hearing,
100   'O may he never more be warm!'
The cold, cold moon above her head,
Thus on her knees did Goody pray,
Young Harry heard what she had said,
And icy-cold he turned away.

He went complaining all the morrow
That he was cold and very chill:
His face was gloom, his heart was sorrow,
Alas! that day for Harry Gill!
That day he wore a riding-coat,
110   But not a whit the warmer he:
Another was on Thursday brought,
And ere the Sabbath he had three.

'Twas all in vain, a useless matter,
And blankets were about him pinn'd;
Yet still his jaws and teeth they clatter,
Like a loose casement in the wind.
And Harry's flesh it fell away;
And all who see him say 'tis plain,
That, live as long as live he may,
120 He never will be warm again.

No word to any man he utters,
A-bed or up, to young or old;
But ever to himself he mutters,
'Poor Harry Gill is very cold.'
A-bed or up, by night or day;
His teeth they chatter, chatter still.
Now think, ye farmers all, I pray,
Of Goody Blake and Harry Gill.

Lines

WRITTEN AT A SMALL DISTANCE FROM MY HOUSE,
AND SENT BY MY LITTLE BOY TO THE PERSON TO
WHOM THEY ARE ADDRESSED

It is the first mild day of March:
Each minute sweeter than before,
The red-breast sings from the tall larch
That stands beside our door.

There is a blessing in the air,
Which seems a sense of joy to yield
To the bare trees, and mountains bare,
And grass in the green field.

My Sister! ('tis a wish of mine)
10   Now that our morning meal is done,
Make haste, your morning task resign;
Come forth and feel the sun.

Edward will come with you, and pray,
Put on with speed your woodland dress,
And bring no book, for this one day
We'll give to idleness.

No joyless forms shall regulate
Our living Calendar:
We from to-day, my friend, will date
20   The opening of the year.

Love, now an universal birth,
From heart to heart is stealing,
From earth to man, from man to earth,
– It is the hour of feeling.

One moment now may give us more
Than fifty years of reason;
Our minds shall drink at every pore
The spirit of the season.

Some silent laws our hearts may make,
30 Which they shall long obey;
We for the year to come may take
Our temper from to-day.

And from the blessed power that rolls
About, below, above;
We'll frame the measure of our souls,
They shall be tuned to love.

Then come, my sister! come, I pray,
With speed put on your woodland dress,
And bring no book; for this one day
40 We'll give to idleness.

Simon Lee, the Old Huntsman

WITH AN INCIDENT IN WHICH HE WAS CONCERNED

In the sweet shire of Cardigan,
Not far from pleasant Ivor-hall,
An old man dwells, a little man,
I've heard he once was tall.
Of years he has upon his back,
No doubt, a burthen weighty;
He says he is three score and ten,
But others say he's eighty.

     A long blue livery-coat has he,
10 That's fair behind, and fair before;
     Yet, meet him where you will, you see
     At once that he is poor.
     Full five and twenty years he lived
     A running huntsman merry;
     And, though he has but one eye left,
     His cheek is like a cherry.

     No man like him the horn could sound,
     And no man was so full of glee;
     To say the least, four counties round
20 Had heard of Simon Lee;
     His master's dead, and no one now
     Dwells in the hall of Ivor;
     Men, dogs, and horses, all are dead;
     He is the sole survivor.

     His hunting feats have him bereft
     Of his right eye, as you may see:
     And then, what limbs those feats have left
     To poor old Simon Lee!
     He has no son, he has no child,
30 His wife, an aged woman,
     Lives with him, near the waterfall,
     Upon the village common.

     And he is lean and he is sick,
     His little body's half awry
     His ancles they are swoln and thick;
     His legs are thin and dry.
     When he was young he little knew
     Of husbandry or tillage;
     And now he's forced to work, though weak,
40   – The weakest in the village.

He all the country could outrun,
Could leave both man and horse behind;
And often, ere the race was done,
He reeled and was stone-blind.
And still there's something in the world
At which his heart rejoices;
For when the chiming hounds are out,
He dearly loves their voices!

Old Ruth works out of doors with him,
50   And does what Simon cannot do;
For she, not over stout of limb,
Is stouter of the two.
And though you with your utmost skill
From labour could not wean them,
Alas! 'tis very little, all
Which they can do between them.

Beside their moss-grown hut of clay,
Not twenty paces from the door,
A scrap of land they have, but they
60   Are poorest of the poor.
This scrap of land he from the heath
Enclosed when he was stronger;
But what avails the land to them,
Which they can till no longer?

Few months of life has he in store,
As he to you will tell,
For still, the more he works, the more
His poor old ancles swell.
My gentle reader, I perceive
70   How patiently you've waited,
And I'm afraid that you expect
Some tale will be related.

O reader! had you in your mind
Such stores as silent thought can bring,
O gentle reader! you would find
A tale in every thing.
What more I have to say is short,
I hope you'll kindly take it;
It is no tale; but should you think,
80 Perhaps a tale you'll make it.

One summer-day I chanced to see
This old man doing all he could
About the root of an old tree,
A stump of rotten wood.
The mattock totter'd in his hand;
So vain was his endeavour
That at the root of the old tree
He might have worked for ever.

'You're overtasked, good Simon Lee,
90 Give me your tool' to him I said;
And at the word right gladly he
Received my proffer'd aid.
I struck, and with a single blow
The tangled root I sever'd,
At which the poor old man so long
And vainly had endeavour'd.

The tears into his eyes were brought,
And thanks and praises seemed to run
So fast out of his heart, I thought
100 They never would have done.
– I've heard of hearts unkind, kind deeds
With coldness still returning.
Alas! the gratitude of men
Has oftner left me mourning.

Anecdote for Fathers

SHEWING HOW THE ART OF LYING MAY BE TAUGHT

I have a boy of five years old,
His face is fair and fresh to see;
His limbs are cast in beauty's mould,
And dearly he loves me.

One morn we stroll'd on our dry walk,
Our quiet house all full in view,
And held such intermitted talk
As we are wont to do.

My thoughts on former pleasures ran;
10   I thought of Kilve's delightful shore,
My pleasant home, when spring began,
A long, long year before.

A day it was when I could bear
To think, and think, and think again;
With so much happiness to spare,
I could not feel a pain.

My boy was by my side, so slim
And graceful in his rustic dress!
And oftentimes I talked to him,
20   In very idleness.

The young lambs ran a pretty race;
The morning sun shone bright and warm;
'Kilve,' said I, 'was a pleasant place,
'And so is Liswyn farm.

'My little boy, which like you more,'
I said and took him by the arm –
'Our home by Kilve's delightful shore,
'Or here at Liswyn farm?'

'And tell me, had you rather be,'
30 I said and held him by the arm,
'At Kilve's smooth shore by the green sea,
'Or here at Liswyn farm?

In careless mood he looked at me,
While still I held him by the arm,
And said, 'At Kilve I'd rather be
'Than here at Liswyn farm.'

'Now, little Edward, say why so;
My little Edward, tell me why;'
'I cannot tell, I do not know.'
40 'Why this is strange,' said I.

'For, here are woods and green-hills warm;
'There surely must some reason be
'Why you would change sweet Liswyn farm
'For Kilve by the green sea.'

At this, my boy, so fair and slim,
Hung down his head, nor made reply;
And five times did I say to him,
'Why? Edward, tell me why?'

His head he raised – there was in sight,
50 It caught his eye, he saw it plain –
Upon the house-top, glittering bright,
A broad and gilded vane.

Then did the boy his tongue unlock,
And thus to me he made reply;
'At Kilve there was no weather-cock,
'And that's the reason why.'

O dearest, dearest boy! my heart
For better lore would seldom yearn,
Could I but teach the hundredth part
60 Of what from thee I learn.

We Are Seven

A simple child, dear brother Jim,
That lightly draws its breath,
And feels its life in every limb,
What should it know of death?

I met a little cottage girl,
She was eight years old, she said;
Her hair was thick with many a curl
That cluster'd round her head.

She had a rustic, woodland air,
10 And she was wildly clad;
Her eyes were fair, and very fair,
– Her beauty made me glad.

'Sisters and brothers, little maid,
'How many may you be?'
'How many? seven in all,' she said,
And wondering looked at me.

'And where are they, I pray you tell?'
She answered, 'Seven are we,
'And two of us at Conway dwell,
20 'And two are gone to sea.

'Two of us in the church-yard lie,
'My sister and my brother,
'And in the church-yard cottage, I
'Dwell near them with my mother.'

'You say that two at Conway dwell,
'And two are gone to sea,
'Yet you are seven; I pray you tell
'Sweet Maid, how this may be?'

Then did the little Maid reply,
30 'Seven boys and girls are we;
'Two of us in the church-yard lie,
'Beneath the church-yard tree.'

'You run about, my little maid,
'Your limbs they are alive;
'If two are in the church-yard laid,
'Then ye are only five.'

'Their graves are green, they may be seen,'
The little Maid replied,
'Twelve steps or more from my mother's door,
40 'And they are side by side.

'My stockings there I often knit,
'My 'kerchief there I hem;
'And there upon the ground I sit –
'I sit and sing to them.

'And often after sunset, Sir,
'When it is light and fair,
'I take my little porringer,
'And eat my supper there.

'The first that died was little Jane;
50   'In bed she moaning lay,
'Till God released her of her pain,
'And then she went away.

'So in the church-yard she was laid,
'And all the summer dry,
'Together round her grave we played,
'My brother John and I.

'And when the ground was white with snow,
'And I could run and slide,
'My brother John was forced to go,
60   'And he lies by her side.'

'How many are you then,' said I,
'If they two are in Heaven?'
The little Maiden did reply,
'O Master! we are seven.'

'But they are dead; those two are dead!
'Their spirits are in heaven!'
'Twas throwing words away; for still
The little Maid would have her will,
And said, 'Nay, we are seven!'

Lines Written in Early Spring

I heard a thousand blended notes,
While in a grove I sate reclined,
In that sweet mood when pleasant thoughts
Bring sad thoughts to the mind.

To her fair works did nature link
The human soul that through me ran;
And much it griev'd my heart to think
What man has made of man.

Through primrose-tufts, in that sweet bower,
10 The periwinkle trail'd its wreathes;
And 'tis my faith that every flower
Enjoys the air it breathes.

The birds around me hopp'd and play'd:
Their thoughts I cannot measure,
But the least motion which they made,
It seem'd a thrill of pleasure.

The budding twigs spread out their fan,
To catch the breezy air;
And I must think, do all I can,
20 That there was pleasure there.

If I these thoughts may not prevent,
If such be of my creed the plan,
Have I not reason to lament
What man has made of man?

The Thorn

I
There is a thorn; it looks so old,
In truth you'd find it hard to say,
How it could ever have been young,
It looks so old and grey.
Not higher than a two-years' child,
It stands erect this aged thorn;
No leaves it has, no thorny points;
It is a mass of knotted joints,
A wretched thing forlorn.
10 It stands erect, and like a stone
With lichens it is overgrown.

II
Like rock or stone, it is o'ergrown
With lichens to the very top,
And hung with heavy tufts of moss,
A melancholy crop:
Up from the earth these mosses creep,
And this poor thorn they clasp it round
So close, you'd say that they were bent
With plain and manifest intent,
20 To drag it to the ground;
And all had joined in one endeavour
To bury this poor thorn for ever.

III
High on a mountain's highest ridge,
Where oft the stormy winter gale
Cuts like a scythe, while through the clouds
It sweeps from vale to vale;
Not five yards from the mountain-path,

75

This thorn you on your left espy;
And to the left, three yards beyond,
30   You see a little muddy pond
Of water, never dry;
I've measured it from side to side:
'Tis three feet long, and two feet wide.

IV
And close beside this aged thorn,
There is a fresh and lovely sight,
A beauteous heap, a hill of moss,
Just half a foot in height.
All lovely colours there you see,
All colours that were ever seen,
40   And mossy network too is there,
As if by hand of lady fair
The work had woven been,
And cups, the darlings of the eye,
So deep is their vermilion dye.

V
Ah me! what lovely tints are there!
Of olive-green and scarlet bright,
In spikes, in branches, and in stars,
Green, red, and pearly white.
This heap of earth o'ergrown with moss,
50   Which close beside the thorn you see,
So fresh in all its beauteous dyes,
Is like an infant's grave in size
As like as like can be:
But never, never any where,
An infant's grave was half so fair.

VI
Now would you see this aged thorn,
This pond and beauteous hill of moss,
You must take care and chuse your time
The mountain when to cross.
60   For oft there sits, between the heap
That's like an infant's grave in size,
And that same pond of which I spoke,
A woman in a scarlet cloak,
And to herself she cries,
'Oh misery! oh misery!
'Oh woe is me! oh misery!'

VII
At all times of the day and night
This wretched woman thither goes,
And she is known to every star,
70   And every wind that blows;
And there beside the thorn she sits
When the blue day-light's in the skies,
And when the whirlwind's on the hill,
Or frosty air is keen and still,
And to herself she cries,
'Oh misery! oh misery!
'Oh woe is me! oh misery!'

VIII
'Now wherefore thus, by day and night,
'In rain, in tempest, and in snow,
80   'Thus to the dreary mountain-top
'Does this poor woman go?
'And why sits she beside the thorn
'When the blue day-light's in the sky,
'Or when the whirlwind's on the hill,
'Or frosty air is keen and still,

'And wherefore does she cry? –
'Oh wherefore? wherefore? tell me why
'Does she repeat that doleful cry?'

IX

I cannot tell; I wish I could;
90 For the true reason no one knows,
But if you'd gladly view the spot,
The spot to which she goes;
The heap that's like an infant's grave,
The pond – and thorn, so old and grey,
Pass by her door – 'tis seldom shut –
And if you see her in her hut,
Then to the spot away! –
I never heard of such as dare
Approach the spot when she is there.

X

100 'But wherefore to the mountain-top
'Can this unhappy woman go,
'Whatever star is in the skies,
'Whatever wind may blow?'
Nay rack your brain – 'tis all in vain,
I'll tell you every thing I know;
But to the thorn, and to the pond
Which is a little step beyond,
I wish that you would go:
Perhaps when you are at the place
110 You something of her tale may trace.

XI

I'll give you the best help I can:
Before you up the mountain go,
Up to the dreary mountain-top,
I'll tell you all I know.

'Tis now some two and twenty years,
Since she (her name is Martha Ray)
Gave with a maiden's true good will
Her company to Stephen Hill;
And she was blithe and gay,
120 And she was happy, happy still
Whene'er she thought of Stephen Hill.

XII
And they had fix'd the wedding-day,
The morning that must wed them both;
But Stephen to another maid
Had sworn another oath;
And with this other maid to church
Unthinking Stephen went –
Poor Martha! on that woful day
A cruel, cruel fire, they say,
130 Into her bones was sent:
It dried her body like a cinder,
And almost turn'd her brain to tinder.

XIII
They say, full six months after this,
While yet the summer-leaves were green,
She to the mountain-top would go,
And there was often seen.
'Tis said, a child was in her womb,
As now to any eye was plain;
She was with child, and she was mad,
140 Yet often she was sober sad
From her exceeding pain.
Oh me! ten thousand times I'd rather
That he had died, that cruel father!

XIV
Sad case for such a brain to hold
Communion with a stirring child!
Sad case, as you may think, for one
Who had a brain so wild!
Last Christmas when we talked of this,
Old Farmer Simpson did maintain,
150 That in her womb the infant wrought
About its mother's heart, and brought
Her senses back again:
And when at last her time drew near,
Her looks were calm, her senses clear.

XV
No more I know, I wish I did,
And I would tell it all to you;
For what became of this poor child
There's none that ever knew:
And if a child was born or no,
160 There's no one that could ever tell;
And if 'twas born alive or dead,
There's no one knows, as I have said,
But some remember well,
That Martha Ray about this time
Would up the mountain often climb.

XVI
And all that winter, when at night
The wind blew from the mountain-peak,
'Twas worth your while, though in the dark,
The church-yard path to seek:
170 For many a time and oft were heard
Cries coming from the mountain-head,
Some plainly living voices were,
And others, I've heard many swear,

Were voices of the dead:
I cannot think, whate'er they say,
They had to do with Martha Ray.

XVII
But that she goes to this old thorn,
The thorn which I've described to you,
And there sits in a scarlet cloak,
180   I will be sworn is true.
For one day with my telescope,
To view the ocean wide and bright,
When to this country first I came,
Ere I had heard of Martha's name,
I climbed the mountain's height:
A storm came on, and I could see
No object higher than my knee.

XVIII
'Twas mist and rain, and storm and rain,
No screen, no fence could I discover,
190   And then the wind! in faith, it was
A wind full ten times over.
I looked around, I thought I saw
A jutting crag, and off I ran,
Head-foremost, through the driving rain,
The shelter of the crag to gain,
And, as I am a man,
Instead of jutting crag, I found
A woman seated on the ground.

XIX
I did not speak – I saw her face,
200   Her face it was enough for me;
I turned about and heard her cry,
'O misery! O misery!'

And there she sits, until the moon
Through half the clear blue sky will go,
And when the little breezes make
The waters of the pond to shake,
As all the country know,
She shudders and you hear her cry,
'Oh misery! oh misery!'

XX

210 'But what's the thorn? and what's the pond?
'And what's the hill of moss to her?
'And what's the creeping breeze that comes
'The little pond to stir?'
I cannot tell; but some will say
She hanged her baby on the tree,
Some say she drowned it in the pond,
Which is a little step beyond,
But all and each agree,
The little babe was buried there,
220 Beneath that hill of moss so fair.

XXI

I've heard the scarlet moss is red
With drops of that poor infant's blood;
But kill a new-born infant thus!
I do not think she could.
Some say, if to the pond you go,
And fix on it a steady view,
The shadow of a babe you trace,
A baby and a baby's face,
And that it looks at you;
230 Whene'er you look on it, 'tis plain
The baby looks at you again.

XXII
And some had sworn an oath that she
Should be to public justice brought;
And for the little infant's bones
With spades they would have sought.
But then the beauteous hill of moss
Before their eyes began to stir;
And for full fifty yards around,
The grass it shook upon the ground;
240 But all do still aver
The little babe is buried there,
Beneath that hill of moss so fair.

XXIII
I cannot tell how this may be,
But plain it is, the thorn is bound
With heavy tufts of moss, that strive
To drag it to the ground.
And this I know, full many a time,
When she was on the mountain high,
By day, and in the silent night,
250 When all the stars shone clear and bright,
That I have heard her cry,
'Oh misery! oh misery!
'O woe is me! oh misery!'

The Last of the Flock

In distant countries I have been,
And yet I have not often seen
A healthy man, a man full grown,
Weep in the public roads alone.
But such a one, on English ground,

And in the broad high-way, I met;
Along the broad high-way he came,
His cheeks with tears were wet.
Sturdy he seemed, though he was sad;
10   And in his arms a lamb he had.

He saw me, and he turned aside,
As if he wished himself to hide:
Then with his coat he made essay
To wipe those briny tears away.
I follow'd him, and said, 'My friend
'What ails you? wherefore weep you so?'
– 'Shame on me, Sir! this lusty lamb,
He makes my tears to flow.
To-day I fetched him from the rock;
20   He is the last of all my flock.

When I was young, a single man,
And after youthful follies ran,
Though little given to care and thought,
Yet, so it was, a ewe I bought;
And other sheep from her I raised,
As healthy sheep as you might see,
And then I married, and was rich
As I could wish to be;
Of sheep I number'd a full score,
30   And every year encreas'd my store.

Year after year my stock it grew,
And from this one, this single ewe,
Full fifty comely sheep I raised,
As sweet a flock as ever grazed!
Upon the mountain did they feed;
They throve, and we at home did thrive.
– This lusty lamb of all my store

Is all that is alive:
And now I care not if we die,
40   And perish all of poverty.

Ten children, Sir! had I to feed,
Hard labour in a time of need!
My pride was tamed, and in our grief
I of the parish ask'd relief.
They said I was a wealthy man;
My sheep upon the mountain fed,
And it was fit that thence I took
Whereof to buy us bread:
'Do this; how can we give to you,'
50   They cried, 'what to the poor is due?'

I sold a sheep as they had said,
And bought my little children bread,
And they were healthy with their food;
For me it never did me good.
A woeful time it was for me,
To see the end of all my gains,
The pretty flock which I had reared
With all my care and pains,
To see it melt like snow away!
60   For me it was a woeful day.

Another still! and still another!
A little lamb, and then its mother!
It was a vein that never stopp'd,
Like blood-drops from my heart they dropp'd.
Till thirty were not left alive
They dwindled, dwindled, one by one,
And I may say that many a time
I wished they all were gone:

They dwindled one by one away;
70 For me it was a woeful day.

To wicked deeds I was inclined,
And wicked fancies cross'd my mind,
And every man I chanc'd to see,
I thought he knew some ill of me.
No peace, no comfort could I find,
No ease, within doors or without,
And crazily, and wearily,
I went my work about.
Oft-times I thought to run away;
80 For me it was a woeful day.

Sir! 'twas a precious flock to me,
As dear as my own children be;
For daily with my growing store
I loved my children more and more.
Alas! it was an evil time;
God cursed me in my sore distress,
I prayed, yet every day I thought
I loved my children less;
And every week, and every day,
90 My flock, it seemed to melt away.

They dwindled, Sir, sad sight to see!
From ten to five, from five to three,
A lamb, a weather, and a ewe;
And then at last, from three to two;
And of my fifty, yesterday
I had but only one,
And here it lies upon my arm,
Alas! and I have none;
To-day I fetched it from the rock;
100 It is the last of all my flock.'

The Dungeon

And this place our forefathers made for man!
This is the process of our love and wisdom,
To each poor brother who offends against us –
Most innocent, perhaps – and what if guilty?
Is this the only cure? Merciful God!
Each pore and natural outlet shrivell'd up
By ignorance and parching poverty,
His energies roll back upon his heart,
And stagnate and corrupt; till changed to poison,
10 They break out on him, like a loathsome plague-spot;
Then we call in our pamper'd mountebanks –
And this is their best cure! uncomforted
And friendless solitude, groaning and tears,
And savage faces, at the clanking hour,
Seen through the steams and vapour of his dungeon,
By the lamp's dismal twilight! So he lies
Circled with evil, till his very soul
Unmoulds its essence, hopelessly deformed
By sights of ever more deformity!

20 With other ministrations thou, O nature!
Healest thy wandering and distempered child:
Thou pourest on him thy soft influences,
Thy sunny hues, fair forms, and breathing sweets,
Thy melodies of woods, and winds, and waters,
Till he relent, and can no more endure
To be a jarring and a dissonant thing,
Amid this general dance and minstrelsy;
But, bursting into tears, wins back his way,
His angry spirit healed and harmonized
30 By the benignant touch of love and beauty.

The Mad Mother

Her eyes are wild, her head is bare,
The sun has burnt her coal-black hair,
Her eye-brows have a rusty stain,
And she came far from over the main.
She has a baby on her arm,
Or else she were alone;
And underneath the hay-stack warm,
And on the green-wood stone,
She talked and sung the woods among;
10 And it was in the English tongue.

'Sweet babe! they say that I am mad,
But nay, my heart is far too glad;
And I am happy when I sing
Full many a sad and doleful thing:
Then, lovely baby, do not fear!
I pray thee have no fear of me,
But, safe as in a cradle, here
My lovely baby! thou shalt be,
To thee I know too much I owe;
20 I cannot work thee any woe.

A fire was once within my brain;
And in my head a dull, dull pain;
And fiendish faces one, two, three,
Hung at my breasts, and pulled at me.
But then there came a sight of joy;
It came at once to do me good;
I waked, and saw my little boy,
My little boy of flesh and blood;
Oh joy for me that sight to see!
30 For he was here, and only he.

Suck, little babe, oh suck again!
It cools my blood; it cools my brain;
Thy lips I feel them, baby! they
Draw from my heart the pain away.
Oh! press me with thy little hand;
It loosens something at my chest;
About that tight and deadly band
I feel thy little fingers press'd.
The breeze I see is in the tree;
40 It comes to cool my babe and me.

Oh! love me, love me, little boy!
Thou art thy mother's only joy;
And do not dread the waves below,
When o'er the sea-rock's edge we go;
The high crag cannot work me harm,
Nor leaping torrents when they howl;
The babe I carry on my arm,
He saves for me my precious soul;
Then happy lie, for blest am I;
50 Without me my sweet babe would die.

Then do not fear, my boy! for thee
Bold as a lion I will be;
And I will always be thy guide,
Through hollow snows and rivers wide.
I'll build an Indian bower; I know
The leaves that make the softest bed:
And if from me thou wilt not go,
But still be true 'till I am dead,
My pretty thing! then thou shalt sing,
60 As merry as the birds in spring.

Thy father cares not for my breast,
'Tis thine, sweet baby, there to rest:
'Tis all thine own! and if its hue
Be changed, that was so fair to view,
'Tis fair enough for thee, my dove!
My beauty, little child, is flown;
But thou wilt live with me in love,
And what if my poor cheek be brown?
'Tis well for me; thou canst not see
70 How pale and wan it else would be.

Dread not their taunts, my little life!
I am thy father's wedded wife;
And underneath the spreading tree
We two will live in honesty.
If his sweet boy he could forsake,
With me he never would have stay'd:
From him no harm my babe can take,
But he, poor man! is wretched made,
And every day we two will pray
80 For him that's gone and far away.

I'll teach my boy the sweetest things;
I'll teach him how the owlet sings.
My little babe! thy lips are still,
And thou hast almost suck'd thy fill.
– Where art thou gone my own dear child?
What wicked looks are those I see?
Alas! alas! that look so wild,
It never, never came from me:
If thou art mad, my pretty lad,
90 Then I must be for ever sad.

Oh! smile on me, my little lamb!
For I thy own dear mother am.
My love for thee has well been tried:
I've sought thy father far and wide.
I know the poisons of the shade,
I know the earth-nuts fit for food;
Then, pretty dear, be not afraid;
We'll find thy father in the wood.
Now laugh and be gay, to the woods away!
100 And there, my babe; we'll live for aye.

The Idiot Boy

'Tis eight o'clock, – a clear March night,
The moon is up – the sky is blue,
The owlet in the moonlight air,
He shouts from nobody knows where;
He lengthens out his lonely shout,
Halloo! halloo! a long halloo!

– Why bustle thus about your door,
What means this bustle, Betty Foy?
Why are you in this mighty fret?
10 And why on horseback have you set
Him whom you love, your idiot boy?

Beneath the moon that shines so bright,
Till she is tired, let Betty Foy
With girt and stirrup fiddle-faddle;
But wherefore set upon a saddle
Him whom she loves, her idiot boy?

There's scarce a soul that's out of bed;
Good Betty! put him down again;
His lips with joy they burr at you,
20 But, Betty! what has he to do
With stirrup, saddle, or with rein?

The world will say 'tis very idle,
Bethink you of the time of night;
There's not a mother, no not one,
But when she hears what you have done,
Oh! Betty she'll be in a fright.

But Betty's bent on her intent,
For her good neighbour, Susan Gale,
Old Susan, she who dwells alone,
30 Is sick, and makes a piteous moan,
As if her very life would fail.

There's not a house within a mile,
No hand to help them in distress:
Old Susan lies a bed in pain,
And sorely puzzled are the twain,
For what she ails they cannot guess.

And Betty's husband's at the wood,
Where by the week he doth abide,
A woodman in the distant vale;
40 There's none to help poor Susan Gale,
What must be done? what will betide?

And Betty from the lane has fetched
Her pony, that is mild and good,
Whether he be in joy or pain,
Feeding at will along the lane,
Or bringing faggots from the wood.

And he is all in travelling trim,
And by the moonlight, Betty Foy
Has up upon the saddle set,
50 The like was never heard of yet,
Him whom she loves, her idiot boy.

And he must post without delay
Across the bridge that's in the dale,
And by the church, and o'er the down,
To bring a doctor from the town,
Or she will die, old Susan Gale.

There is no need of boot or spur,
There is no need of whip or wand,
For Johnny has his holly-bough,
60 And with a hurly-burly now
He shakes the green bough in his hand.

And Betty o'er and o'er has told
The boy who is her best delight,
Both what to follow, what to shun,
What do, and what to leave undone,
How turn to left, and how to right.

And Betty's most especial charge,
Was, 'Johnny! Johnny! mind that you
'Come home again, nor stop at all,
70 'Come home again, whate'er befal,
'My Johnny do, I pray you do.'

To this did Johnny answer make,
Both with his head, and with his hand,
And proudly shook the bridle too,
And then! his words were not a few,
Which Betty well could understand.

And now that Johnny is just going,
Though Betty's in a mighty flurry,
She gently pats the pony's side,
80   On which her idiot boy must ride,
And seems no longer in a hurry.

But when the pony moved his legs,
Oh! then for the poor idiot boy!
For joy he cannot hold the bridle,
For joy his head and heels are idle,
He's idle all for very joy.

And while the pony moves his legs,
In Johnny's left-hand you may see,
The green bough's motionless and dead;
90   The moon that shines above his head
Is not more still and mute than he.

His heart it was so full of glee,
That till full fifty yards were gone,
He quite forgot his holly whip,
And all his skill in horsemanship,
Oh! happy, happy, happy John.

And Betty's standing at the door,
And Betty's face with joy o'erflows,
Proud of herself, and proud of him,
100   She sees him in his travelling trim;
How quietly her Johnny goes.

The silence of her idiot boy,
What hopes it sends to Betty's heart!
He's at the guide-post – he turns right,
She watches till he's out of sight,
And Betty will not then depart.

Burr, burr – now Johnny's lips they burr,
As loud as any mill, or near it,
Meek as a lamb the pony moves,
110 And Johnny makes the noise he loves,
And Betty listens, glad to hear it.

Away she hies to Susan Gale:
And Johnny's in a merry tune,
The owlets hoot, the owlets curr,
And Johnny's lips they burr, burr, burr,
And on he goes beneath the moon.

His steed and he right well agree,
For of this pony there's a rumour,
That should he lose his eyes and ears,
120 And should he live a thousand years,
He never will be out of humour.

But then he is a horse that thinks!
And when he thinks his pace is slack;
Now, though he knows poor Johnny well,
Yet for his life he cannot tell
What he has got upon his back.

So through the moonlight lanes they go,
And far into the moonlight dale,
And by the church, and o'er the down,
130 To bring a doctor from the town,
To comfort poor old Susan Gale.

And Betty, now at Susan's side,
Is in the middle of her story,
What comfort Johnny soon will bring,
With many a most diverting thing,
Of Johnny's wit and Johnny's glory.

And Betty's still at Susan's side:
By this time she's not quite so flurried;
Demure with porringer and plate
140 She sits, as if in Susan's fate
Her life and soul were buried.

But Betty, poor good woman! she,
You plainly in her face may read it,
Could lend out of that moment's store
Five years of happiness or more,
To any that might need it.

But yet I guess that now and then
With Betty all was not so well,
And to the road she turns her ears,
150 And thence full many a sound she hears,
Which she to Susan will not tell.

Poor Susan moans, poor Susan groans,
'As sure as there's a moon in heaven,'
Cries Betty, 'he'll be back again;
'They'll both be here, 'tis almost ten,
'They'll both be here before eleven.'

Poor Susan moans, poor Susan groans,
The clock gives warning for eleven;
'Tis on the stroke – 'If Johnny's near,'
160 Quoth Betty 'he will soon be here,
'As sure as there's a moon in heaven.'

The clock is on the stroke of twelve,
And Johnny is not yet in sight,
The moon's in heaven, as Betty sees,
But Betty is not quite at ease;
And Susan has a dreadful night.

And Betty, half an hour ago,
On Johnny vile reflections cast;
'A little idle sauntering thing!'
170 With other names, an endless string,
But now that time is gone and past.

And Betty's drooping at the heart,
That happy time all past and gone,
'How can it be he is so late?
'The doctor he has made him wait,
'Susan! they'll both be here anon.'

And Susan's growing worse and worse,
And Betty's in a sad quandary;
And then there's nobody to say
180 If she must go or she must stay;
– She's in a sad quandary.

The clock is on the stroke of one;
But neither Doctor nor his guide
Appear along the moonlight road,
There's neither horse nor man abroad,
And Betty's still at Susan's side.

And Susan she begins to fear
Of sad mischances not a few,
That Johnny may perhaps be drown'd,
190 Or lost perhaps, and never found;
Which they must both for ever rue.

She prefaced half a hint of this
With, 'God forbid it should be true!'
At the first word that Susan said
Cried Betty, rising from the bed,
'Susan, I'd gladly stay with you.

'I must be gone, I must away,
'Consider, Johnny's but half-wise;
'Susan, we must take care of him,
200 'If he is hurt in life or limb' –
'Oh God forbid!' poor Susan cries.

'What can I do?' says Betty, going,
'What can I do to ease your pain?
'Good Susan tell me, and I'll stay;
'I fear you're in a dreadful way,
'But I shall soon be back again.'

'Good Betty go, good Betty go,
'There's nothing that can ease my pain.'
Then off she hies, but with a prayer
210 That God poor Susan's life would spare,
Till she comes back again.

So, through the moonlight lane she goes,
And far into the moonlight dale;
And how she ran, and how she walked,
And all that to herself she talked,
Would surely be a tedious tale.

In high and low, above, below,
In great and small, in round and square,
In tree and tower was Johnny seen,
220 In bush and brake, in black and green,
'Twas Johnny, Johnny, every where.

She's past the bridge that's in the dale,
And now the thought torments her sore,
Johnny perhaps his horse forsook,
To hunt the moon that's in the brook,
And never will be heard of more.

And now she's high upon the down,
Alone amid a prospect wide;
There's neither Johnny nor his horse,
230 Among the fern or in the gorse;
There's neither doctor nor his guide.

'Oh saints! what is become of him?
'Perhaps he's climbed into an oak,
'Where he will stay till he is dead;
'Or sadly he has been misled,
'And joined the wandering gypsey-folk.

'Or him that wicked pony's carried
'To the dark cave, the goblins' hall,
'Or in the castle he's pursuing,
240 'Among the ghosts, his own undoing;
'Or playing with the waterfall.'

At poor old Susan then she railed,
While to the town she posts away;
'If Susan had not been so ill,
'Alas! I should have had him still,
'My Johnny, till my dying day.'

Poor Betty! in this sad distemper,
The doctor's self would hardly spare,
Unworthy things she talked and wild,
250 Even he, of cattle the most mild,
The pony had his share.

And now she's got into the town,
And to the doctor's door she hies;
'Tis silence all on every side;
The town so long, the town so wide,
Is silent as the skies.

And now she's at the doctor's door,
She lifts the knocker, rap, rap, rap,
The doctor at the casement shews,
His glimmering eyes that peep and doze;
And one hand rubs his old night-cap.

'Oh Doctor! Doctor! where's my Johnny?'
'I'm here, what is't you want with me?'
'Oh Sir! you know I'm Betty Foy,
'And I have lost my poor dear boy,
'You know him – him you often see;

'He's not so wise as some folks be,'
'The devil take his wisdom!' said
The Doctor, looking somewhat grim,
'What, woman! should I know of him?'
And, grumbling, he went back to bed.

'O woe is me! O woe is me!
'Here will I die; here will I die;
'I thought to find my Johnny here,
'But he is neither far nor near,
'Oh! what a wretched mother I!'

She stops, she stands, she looks about,
Which way to turn she cannot tell.
Poor Betty! it would ease her pain
If she had heart to knock again;
– The clock strikes three – a dismal knell!

Then up along the town she hies,
No wonder if her senses fail,
This piteous news so much it shock'd her,
She quite forgot to send the Doctor,
To comfort poor old Susan Gale.

And now she's high upon the down,
And she can see a mile of road,
'Oh cruel! I'm almost three-score;
290 'Such night as this was ne'er before,
'There's not a single soul abroad.'

She listens, but she cannot hear
The foot of horse, the voice of man;
The streams with softest sound are flowing,
The grass you almost hear it growing,
You hear it now if e'er you can.

The owlets through the long blue night
Are shouting to each other still:
Fond lovers, yet not quite hob nob,
300 They lengthen out the tremulous sob,
That echoes far from hill to hill.

Poor Betty now has lost all hope,
Her thoughts are bent on deadly sin;
A green-grown pond she just has pass'd,
And from the brink she hurries fast,
Lest she should drown herself therein.

And now she sits her down and weeps;
Such tears she never shed before;
'Oh dear, dear pony! my sweet joy!
310 'Oh carry back my idiot boy!
'And we will ne'er o'erload thee more.'

A thought is come into her head;
'The pony he is mild and good,
'And we have always used him well;
'Perhaps he's gone along the dell,
'And carried Johnny to the wood.'

Then up she springs as if on wings;
She thinks no more of deadly sin;
If Betty fifty ponds should see,
320 The last of all her thoughts would be,
To drown herself therein.

Oh reader! now that I might tell
What Johnny and his horse are doing!
What they've been doing all this time,
Oh could I put it into rhyme,
A most delightful tale pursuing!

Perhaps, and no unlikely thought!
He with his pony now doth roam
The cliffs and peaks so high that are,
330 To lay his hands upon a star,
And in his pocket bring it home.

Perhaps he's turned himself about,
His face unto his horse's tail,
And still and mute, in wonder lost,
All like a silent horseman-ghost,
He travels on along the vale.

And now, perhaps, he's hunting sheep,
A fierce and dreadful hunter he!
Yon valley, that's so trim and green,
340 In five months' time, should he be seen,
A desart wilderness will be.

Perhaps, with head and heels on fire,
And like the very soul of evil,
He's galloping away, away,
And so he'll gallop on for aye,
The bane of all that dread the devil.

I to the muses have been bound,
These fourteen years, by strong indentures;
Oh gentle muses! let me tell
350   But half of what to him befel,
For sure he met with strange adventures.

Oh gentle muses! is this kind?
Why will ye thus my suit repel?
Why of your further aid bereave me?
And can ye thus unfriended leave me?
Ye muses! whom I love so well.

Who's yon, that, near the waterfall,
Which thunders down with headlong force,
Beneath the moon, yet shining fair,
360   As careless as if nothing were,
Sits upright on a feeding horse?

Unto his horse, that's feeding free,
He seems, I think, the rein to give;
Of moon or stars he takes no heed;
Of such we in romances read,
– 'Tis Johnny! Johnny! as I live.

And that's the very pony too.
Where is she, where is Betty Foy?
She hardly can sustain her fears;
370   The roaring water-fall she hears,
And cannot find her idiot boy.

Your pony's worth his weight in gold,
Then calm your terrors, Betty Foy!
She's coming from among the trees,
And now, all full in view, she sees
Him whom she loves, her idiot boy.

And Betty sees the pony too:
Why stand you thus Good Betty Foy?
It is no goblin, 'tis no ghost,
380   'Tis he whom you so long have lost,
He whom you love, your idiot boy.

She looks again – her arms are up –
She screams – she cannot move for joy;
She darts as with a torrent's force,
She almost has o'erturned the horse,
And fast she holds her idiot boy.

And Johnny burrs and laughs aloud,
Whether in cunning or in joy,
I cannot tell; but while he laughs,
390   Betty a drunken pleasure quaffs,
To hear again her idiot boy.

And now she's at the pony's tail,
And now she's at the pony's head,
On that side now, and now on this,
And almost stifled with her bliss,
A few sad tears does Betty shed.

She kisses o'er and o'er again,
Him whom she loves, her idiot boy,
She's happy here, she's happy there,
400   She is uneasy every where;
Her limbs are all alive with joy.

She pats the pony, where or when
She knows not, happy Betty Foy!
The little pony glad may be,
But he is milder far than she,
You hardly can perceive his joy.

'Oh! Johnny, never mind the Doctor;
'You've done your best, and that is all.'
She took the reins, when this was said,
410 And gently turned the pony's head
From the loud water-fall.

By this the stars were almost gone,
The moon was setting on the hill,
So pale you scarcely looked at her:
The little birds began to stir,
Though yet their tongues were still.

The pony, Betty, and her boy,
Wind slowly through the woody dale:
And who is she, be-times abroad,
420 That hobbles up the steep rough road?
Who is it, but old Susan Gale?

Long Susan lay deep lost in thought,
And many dreadful fears beset her,
Both for her messenger and nurse;
And as her mind grew worse and worse,
Her body it grew better.

She turned, she toss'd herself in bed,
On all sides doubts and terrors met her;
Point after point did she discuss;
430 And while her mind was fighting thus,
Her body still grew better.

'Alas! what is become of them?
'These fears can never be endured,
'I'll to the wood.' – The word scarce said,
Did Susan rise up from her bed,
As if by magic cured.

Away she posts up hill and down,
And to the wood at length is come,
She spies her friends, she shouts a greeting;
440 Oh me! it is a merry meeting,
As ever was in Christendom.

The owls have hardly sung their last,
While our four travellers homeward wend;
The owls have hooted all night long,
And with the owls began my song,
And with the owls must end.

For while they all were travelling home,
Cried Betty, 'Tell us Johnny, do,
'Where all this long night you have been,
450 'What you have heard, what you have seen,
'And Johnny, mind you tell us true.'

Now Johnny all night long had heard
The owls in tuneful concert strive;
No doubt too he the moon had seen;
For in the moonlight he had been
From eight o'clock till five.

And thus to Betty's question, he
Made answer, like a traveller bold,
(His very words I give to you,)
460 'The cocks did crow to-whoo, to-whoo,
'And the sun did shine so cold.'
– Thus answered Johnny in his glory,
And that was all his travel's story.

Lines Written near Richmond, upon the Thames, at Evening

How rich the wave, in front, imprest
With evening-twilight's summer hues,
While, facing thus the crimson west,
The boat her silent path pursues!
And see how dark the backward stream!
A little moment past, so smiling!
And still, perhaps, with faithless gleam,
Some other loiterer beguiling.

Such views the youthful bard allure,
But, heedless of the following gloom,
He deems their colours shall endure
'Till peace go with him to the tomb.
– And let him nurse his fond deceit,
And what if he must die in sorrow!
Who would not cherish dreams so sweet,
Though grief and pain may come to-morrow?

Glide gently, thus for ever glide,
O Thames! that other bards may see,
As lovely visions by thy side
As now, fair river! come to me.
Oh glide, fair stream! for ever so;
Thy quiet soul on all bestowing,
'Till all our minds for ever flow,
As thy deep waters now are flowing.

Vain thought! yet be as now thou art,
That in thy waters may be seen
The image of a poet's heart,
How bright, how solemn, how serene!

Such heart did once the poet bless,
30 Who, pouring here a* *later* ditty,
Could find no refuge from distress,
But in the milder grief of pity.

Remembrance! as we glide along,
For him suspend the dashing oar,
And pray that never child of Song
May know his freezing sorrows more.
How calm! how still! the only sound,
The dripping of the oar suspended!
– The evening darkness gathers round
40 By virtue's holiest powers attended.

Expostulation and Reply

'Why William, on that old grey stone,
'Thus for the length of half a day,
'Why William, sit you thus alone,
'And dream your time away?

'Where are your books? that light bequeath'd
'To beings else forlorn and blind!
'Up! Up! and drink the spirit breath'd
'From dead men to their kind.

'You look round on your mother earth,
10 'As if she for no purpose bore you;
'As if you were her first-born birth,
'And none had lived before you!'

---

* Collins's *Ode on the death of Thomson*, the last written, I believe, of the poems wh
were published during his lifetime. This Ode is also alluded to in the next stanza.

One morning thus, by Esthwaite lake,
When life was sweet I knew not why,
To me my good friend Matthew spake,
And thus I made reply.

'The eye it cannot chuse but see,
'We cannot bid the ear be still;
'Our bodies feel, where'er they be,
20   'Against, or with our will

'Nor less I deem that there are powers,
'Which of themselves our minds impress,
'That we can feed this mind of ours,
'In a wise passiveness.

'Think you, mid all this mighty sum
'Of things for ever speaking,
'That nothing of itself will come,
'But we must still be seeking?

'– Then ask not wherefore, here, alone,
30   'Conversing as I may,
'I sit upon this old grey stone,
'And dream my time away.'

The Tables Turned

AN EVENING SCENE, ON THE SAME SUBJECT

Up! up! my friend, and clear your looks,
Why all this toil and trouble?
Up! up! my friend, and quit your books,
Or surely you'll grow double.

The sun above the mountain's head,
A freshening lustre mellow,
Through all the long green fields has spread,
His first sweet evening yellow.

Books! 'tis a dull and endless strife,
10 Come, hear the woodland linnet,
How sweet his music; on my life
There's more of wisdom in it.

And hark! how blithe the throstle sings!
And he is no mean preacher;
Come forth into the light of things,
Let Nature be your teacher.

She has a world of ready wealth,
Our minds and hearts to bless –
Spontaneous wisdom breathed by health,
20 Truth breathed by chearfulness.

One impulse from a vernal wood
May teach you more of man;
Of moral evil and of good,
Than all the sages can.

Sweet is the lore which nature brings;
Our meddling intellect
Mis-shapes the beauteous forms of things;
– We murder to dissect.

Enough of science and of art;
30 Close up these barren leaves;
Come forth, and bring with you a heart
That watches and receives.

Old Man Travelling

ANIMAL TRANQUILLITY AND DECAY, A SKETCH

        The little hedge-row birds,
That peck along the road, regard him not.
He travels on, and in his face, his step,
His gait, is one expression; every limb,
His look and bending figure, all bespeak
A man who does not move with pain, but moves
With thought – He is insensibly subdued
To settled quiet: he is one by whom
All effort seems forgotten, one to whom
Long patience has such mild composure given,
That patience now doth seem a thing, of which
He hath no need. He is by nature led
To peace so perfect, that the young behold
With envy, what the old man hardly feels.
– I asked him whither he was bound, and what
The object of his journey; he replied
'Sir! I am going many miles to take
'A last leave of my son, a mariner,
'Who from a sea-fight has been brought to Falmouth,
And there is dying in an hospital.'

The Complaint of a Forsaken Indian Woman

[*When a Northern Indian, from sickness, is unable to continue his journey with his companions; he is left behind, covered over with Deer-skins, and is supplied with water, food, and fuel if the situation of the place will afford it. He is informed of the track which his companions intend to pursue, and if he is unable to follow, or overtake them, he perishes alone in the Desart; unless he should have the good fortune to fall in with some other Tribes of Indians. It is unnecessary to add that the females are equally, or still more, exposed to the same fate. See that very interesting work,* Hearne's Journey *from* Hudson's Bay *to the* Northern Ocean. *When the Northern Lights, as the same writer informs us, vary their position in the air, they make a rustling and a crackling noise. This circumstance is alluded to in the first stanza of the following poem.*]

The Complaint, &c.

Before I see another day,
Oh let my body die away!
In sleep I heard the northern gleams;
The stars they were among my dreams;
In sleep did I behold the skies,
I saw the crackling flashes drive;
And yet they are upon my eyes,
And yet I am alive.
Before I see another day,
10   Oh let my body die away!

My fire is dead: it knew no pain;
Yet is it dead, and I remain.
All stiff with ice the ashes lie;
And they are dead, and I will die.
When I was well, I wished to live,
For clothes, for warmth, for food, and fire;
But they to me no joy can give,
No pleasure now, and no desire.
Then here contented will I lie;
20 Alone I cannot fear to die.

Alas! you might have dragged me on
Another day, a single one!
Too soon despair o'er me prevailed;
Too soon my heartless spirit failed;
When you were gone my limbs were stronger,
And Oh how grievously I rue,
That, afterwards, a little longer,
My friends, I did not follow you!
For strong and without pain I lay,
30 My friends, when you were gone away.

My child! they gave thee to another,
A woman who was not thy mother.
When from my arms my babe they took,
On me how strangely did he look!
Through his whole body something ran,
A most strange something did I see;
– As if he strove to be a man,
That he might pull the sledge for me.
And then he stretched his arms, how wild!
40 Oh mercy! like a little child.

My little joy! my little pride!
In two days more I must have died.
Then do not weep and grieve for me;
I feel I must have died with thee.
Oh wind that o'er my head art flying,
The way my friends their course did bend,
I should not feel the pain of dying,
Could I with thee a message send.
Too soon, my friends, you went away;
50   For I had many things to say.

I'll follow you across the snow,
You travel heavily and slow:
In spite of all my weary pain,
I'll look upon your tents again.
My fire is dead, and snowy white
The water which beside it stood;
The wolf has come to me to-night,
And he has stolen away my food.
For ever left alone am I,
60   Then wherefore should I fear to die?

My journey will be shortly run,
I shall not see another sun,
I cannot lift my limbs to know
If they have any life or no.
My poor forsaken child! if I
For once could have thee close to me,
With happy heart I then would die,
And my last thoughts would happy be.
I feel my body die away,
70   I shall not see another day.

The Convict

The glory of evening was spread through the west;
  – On the slope of a mountain I stood,
While the joy that precedes the calm season of rest
  Rang loud through the meadow and wood.

'And must we then part from a dwelling so fair?'
  In the pain of my spirit I said,
And with a deep sadness I turned, to repair
  To the cell where the convict is laid.

The thick-ribbed walls that o'ershadow the gate
10   Resound; and the dungeons unfold:
I pause; and at length, through the glimmering grate,
  That outcast of pity behold.

His black matted head on his shoulder is bent,
  And deep is the sigh of his breath,
And with stedfast dejection his eyes are intent
  On the fetters that link him to death.

'Tis sorrow enough on that visage to gaze,
  That body dismiss'd from his care;
Yet my fancy has pierced to his heart, and pourtrays
20   More terrible images there.

His bones are consumed, and his life-blood is dried,
  With wishes the past to undo;
And his crime, through the pains that o'erwhelm
    him, descried,
  Still blackens and grows on his view.

When from the dark synod, or blood-reeking field,
    To his chamber the monarch is led,
All soothers of sense their soft virtue shall yield,
    And quietness pillow his head.

But if grief, self-consumed, in oblivion would doze,
30   And conscience her tortures appease,
'Mid tumult and uproar this man must repose;
    In the comfortless vault of disease.

When his fetters at night have so press'd on his limbs,
    That the weight can no longer be borne,
If, while a half-slumber his memory bedims,
    The wretch on his pallet should turn,

While the jail-mastiff howls at the dull clanking chain,
    From the roots of his hair there shall start
A thousand sharp punctures of cold-sweating pain,
40   And terror shall leap at his heart.

But now he half-raises his deep-sunken eye,
    And the motion unsettles a tear;
The silence of sorrow it seems to supply,
    And asks of me why I am here.

'Poor victim! no idle intruder has stood
    'With o'erweening complacence our state to compar
'But one, whose first wish is the wish to be good,
    'Is come as a brother thy sorrows to share.

'At thy name though compassion her nature resign,
50   'Though in virtue's proud mouth thy report be a stai
'My care, if the arm of the mighty were mine,
    'Would plant thee where yet thou might'st blosso
        again.'

Lines Written a Few Miles above Tintern Abbey

ON REVISITING THE BANKS OF THE WYE DURING A
TOUR, JULY 13, 1798

Five years have passed; five summers, with the
    length
Of five long winters! and again I hear
These waters, rolling from their mountain-springs
With a sweet inland murmur.* – Once again
Do I behold these steep and lofty cliffs,
Which on a wild secluded scene impress
Thoughts of more deep seclusion; and connect
The landscape with the quiet of the sky.
The day is come when I again repose

10 Here, under this dark sycamore, and view
These plots of cottage-ground, these orchard-
    tufts,
Which, at this season, with their unripe fruits,
Among the woods and copses lose themselves,
Nor, with their green and simple hue, disturb
The wild green landscape. Once again I see
These hedge-rows, hardly hedge-rows, little lines
Of sportive wood run wild; these pastoral farms
Green to the very door; and wreathes of smoke
Sent up, in silence, from among the trees,

20 With some uncertain notice, as might seem,
Of vagrant dwellers in the houseless woods,
Or of some hermit's cave, where by his fire
The hermit sits alone.

---

* The river is not affected by the tides a few miles above Tintern.

       Though absent long,
These forms of beauty have not been to me,
As is a landscape to a blind man's eye:
But oft, in lonely rooms, and mid the din
Of towns and cities, I have owed to them,
In hours of weariness, sensations sweet,
Felt in the blood, and felt along the heart,
30 And passing even into my purer mind
With tranquil restoration: – feelings too
Of unremembered pleasure; such, perhaps,
As may have had no trivial influence
On that best portion of a good man's life;
His little, nameless, unremembered acts
Of kindness and of love. Nor less, I trust,
To them I may have owed another gift,
Of aspect more sublime; that blessed mood,
In which the burthen of the mystery,
40 In which the heavy and the weary weight
Of all this unintelligible world
Is lighten'd: – that serene and blessed mood,
In which the affections gently lead us on,
Until, the breath of this corporeal frame,
And even the motion of our human blood
Almost suspended, we are laid asleep
In body, and become a living soul:
While with an eye made quiet by the power
Of harmony, and the deep power of joy,
We see into the life of things.

50   If this
Be but a vain belief, yet, oh! how oft,
In darkness, and amid the many shapes
Of joyless day-light; when the fretful stir
Unprofitable, and the fever of the world,

Have hung upon the beatings of my heart,
How oft, in spirit, have I turned to thee
O sylvan Wye! Thou wanderer through the woods,
How often has my spirit turned to thee!

And now, with gleams of half-extinguish'd
    thought,
60 With many recognitions dim and faint,
And somewhat of a sad perplexity,
The picture of the mind revives again:
While here I stand, not only with the sense
Of present pleasure, but with pleasing thoughts
That in this moment there is life and food
For future years. And so I dare to hope
Though changed, no doubt, from what I was, when
    first
I came among these hills; when like a roe
I bounded o'er the mountains, by the sides
70 Of the deep rivers, and the lonely streams,
Wherever nature led; more like a man
Flying from something that he dreads, than one
Who sought the thing he loved. For nature then
(The coarser pleasures of my boyish days,
And their glad animal movements all gone by,)
To me was all in all. – I cannot paint
What then I was. The sounding cataract
Haunted me like a passion: the tall rock,
The mountain, and the deep and gloomy wood,
80 Their colours and their forms, were then to me
An appetite: a feeling and a love,
That had no need of a remoter charm,
By thought supplied, or any interest
Unborrowed from the eye. – That time is past,
And all its aching joys are now no more,

And all its dizzy raptures. Not for this
Faint I, nor mourn nor murmur: other gifts
Have followed, for such loss, I would believe,
Abundant recompence. For I have learned
90 To look on nature, not as in the hour
Of thoughtless youth, but hearing oftentimes
The still, sad music of humanity,
Not harsh nor grating, though of ample power
To chasten and subdue. And I have felt
A presence that disturbs me with the joy
Of elevated thoughts; a sense sublime
Of something far more deeply interfused,
Whose dwelling is the light of setting suns,
And the round ocean, and the living air,
100 And the blue sky, and in the mind of man,
A motion and a spirit, that impels
All thinking things, all objects of all thought,
And rolls through all things. Therefore am I still
A lover of the meadows and the woods,
And mountains; and of all that we behold
From this green earth; of all the mighty world
Of eye and ear, both what they half-create,*
And what perceive; well pleased to recognize
In nature and the language of the sense,
110 The anchor of my purest thoughts, the nurse,
The guide, the guardian of my heart, and soul
Of all my moral being.

    Nor, perchance,
If I were not thus taught, should I the more
Suffer my genial spirits to decay:

---

* This line has a close resemblance to an admirable line of Young, the exact
expression of which I cannot recollect.

For thou art with me, here, upon the banks
Of this fair river; thou, my dearest Friend,
My dear, dear Friend, and in thy voice I catch
The language of my former heart, and read
My former pleasures in the shooting lights
120　Of thy wild eyes. Oh! yet a little while
May I behold in thee what I was once,
My dear, dear Sister! And this prayer I make,
Knowing that Nature never did betray
The heart that loved her; 'tis her privilege,
Through all the years of this our life, to lead
From joy to joy: for she can so inform
The mind that is within us, so impress
With quietness and beauty, and so feed
With lofty thoughts, that neither evil tongues,
130　Rash judgments, nor the sneers of selfish men,
Nor greetings where no kindness is, nor all
The dreary intercourse of daily life,
Shall e'er prevail against us, or disturb
Our chearful faith that all which we behold
Is full of blessings. Therefore let the moon
Shine on thee in thy solitary walk;
And let the misty mountain winds be free
To blow against thee: and in after years,
When these wild ecstasies shall be matured
140　Into a sober pleasure, when thy mind
Shall be a mansion for all lovely forms,
Thy memory be as a dwelling-place
For all sweet sounds and harmonies; Oh! then,
If solitude, or fear, or pain, or grief,
Should be thy portion, with what healing
　　　thoughts
Of tender joy wilt thou remember me,
And these my exhortations! Nor, perchance,

If I should be, where I no more can hear
Thy voice, nor catch from thy wild eyes these
    gleams
150 Of past existence, wilt thou then forget
That on the banks of this delightful stream
We stood together; and that I, so long
A worshipper of Nature, hither came,
Unwearied in that service: rather say
With warmer love, oh! with far deeper zeal
Of holier love. Nor wilt thou then forget,
That after many wanderings, many years
Of absence, these steep woods and lofty cliffs,
And this green pastoral landscape, were to me
160 More dear, both for themselves, and for thy sake.

Notes

Advertisement to the 1798 Edition

The first edition was published anonymously but there is little doubt that the Advertisement was written by Wordsworth. It is a measure of his self-doubt that he needs to explain the purpose of *Lyrical Ballads*, carefully deflecting criticism by describing the collection as an *experiment* designed to avoid *the gaudiness and inane phraseology of many modern writers*. In effect, he aims to break away from the elaborate figures of speech, rhyming couplets and exact metres of the eighteenth century, though he only mentions the escapism and fantasy of the modern novel. He asks the reader to look for *human* and *natural* characterization, appealing to instinct rather than *that most dreadful enemy of our pleasures, our own pre-established codes of decision*. He does not tell us what these codes are. He vouches for the authenticity of the tales fearing they may be thought too extreme.

There is a hint of sarcasm in referring to readers *of superior judgement* schooled in the *Discourses* of Sir Joshua Reynolds. Later critics were to seize on *Lyrical Ballads* as the manifesto of a revolution in literary theory, but it may be salutary to consider that Wordsworth may well be referring to nothing more than a return to the spirit of the Roman poets and historians whom he loved and who believed that poetry should have a social purpose. His explanations are rather vague, indicating why he would later feel the need to consider a more rigorous discussion in his Preface to the 1800 edition. Unlike the latter, the tone of the *Advertisement* seems wary of readers of more *correct* taste. These were the ones who would find the poems homespun and inelegant.

The Rime of the Ancyent Marinere

Coleridge's greatest poem and perhaps the most imaginative of the early Romantic period has achieved the status of what T.S. Eliot held to be the true poetry of genius; work so seminal that it changes all the literature that follows. It is a work of Christian mysticism far more transcendental than anything Wordsworth, even at his most visionary, would achieve. It reflects Coleridge's love of metaphysical speculation and his wide reading of those curious and exotic books that appeal to a man of voracious curiosity and imagination.

The idea was conceived during a walk with Wordsworth over Quantoxhead in November 1797, when England was at war with France and the topic of naval warfare was controversial due to unrest among the sailors pressed into service. Bear in mind that at this time navigation was entirely based on favourable winds. The salvation of England by Nelson's fleet at Trafalgar in 1805 would be hailed as a fulfilment of England's destiny as a naval power as well as an act of God's grace. It was Wordsworth who suggested the story of an old Navigator and the consequences of his killing a sea-bird, for which act he would be punished. Coleridge had long been collecting ideas on such matters as sea voyages, deep-sea spirits, angelic forces, astronomy, madness, dreams – all of which he would weave into a poem about the origins of evil and man's fall from grace. He wished to explore the laws of hospitality, home, obsession and guilt, of man's natural as well as his spiritual life; and into this narrative he would blend images of all the elements – frost and fire, air, sun and water. He would devise a complex time-scheme, divided between the recollections of the Mariner, the reactions of the Wedding Guest and the ceremony of marriage, tying together events *inside* and *outside* the tale.

For Coleridge the supernatural was something not separate from the natural but the inner essence of it. A true Romantic, he was searching for the lost glory before the Fall, and since he would not find it in Pantisocracy, nor in a happy marriage, he was driven to find it in poetry. His ballad was to be a mixture of the Gothic styles of G.A. Burger (*Lenore – a night ride with the devil*) and Monk Lewis; not to emulate Gothic horror but to find a vehicle that discovers divine workings through the experiences of man in nature. The form quickly became more than an imitation of a genre. He refined the traditional ballad form of four-line stanzas into a much more musical unit of four, five and six stresses to the line, achieving a *breathing* line tuned to the voice of the narrator.

The interpretation of the poem should finally be yours, for the poem is so complex a work of the imagination that there can be no definitive view. The notes here take an overtly Christian and mystical line, but there are many possible interpretations and you may wish to see the poem in more human or naturalistic terms. But first you should enjoy the poem simply as an old sailor's story relating natural and supernatural events. Only when you come to study the deeper levels of this unique work will you find the following commentary useful.

Like William Blake, Coleridge created his own metaphysical universe. Any understanding of its complexities is difficult without some idea of what we might call his Transcendental Physiology, and because of its strangeness, he would later, in 1815–1816, add annotations or glosses. The *Argument* mentions the Line (the Equator), the South Pole, and the tropical latitudes of the Great (South) Pacific Ocean. This implies a geographical map and you will have noticed in your first reading how careful Coleridge is to describe places and events in relation to the four poles. The journey is also spiritual and elemental. He frequently refers to the four elements and these, in turn, are related to a threefold concept of man as body, soul and spirit – body being the purely material life, soul the sentient being connected with water and all that flows, air a manifestation of God's spirit and of angelic powers, and fire a two-fold quality – heat in its evil manifestation and light in its sacred one.

As if this is not complex enough, Coleridge also employs ideas from a number of religious mystics and alchemists, particularly the Cabbalistic writings of Emanuel Swedenborg

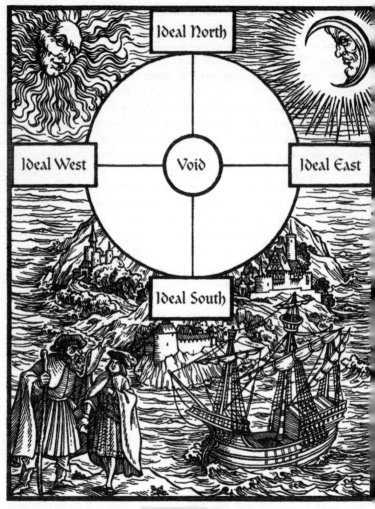

Void Area unprotected by Nature
North Magnetic pole, home, family, marriage, human love, grace
South Polar spirit, suspension of sentient life, death
West Setting sun, heat, lower senses, unreality, damnation
East Rising sun, light, higher senses, reality, redemption through Christ

(1688–1772) and Jacob Boehme (1575–1624). Boehme's *The Aurora*, translated from the German by William Law (4 vols, 1764–1781), in which he explains his view of creation as being produced from light, was one of Coleridge's precious texts. Coleridge's copy, now in the British Museum, is copiously annotated. Alchemy and Hermetic texts (from the mystic Hermes Trismegistus) provided him with a set of symbols which acted *to prevent my mind from being imprisoned within the outline of any single dogmatic system. They contributed to keep alive the heart in the head; gave me an indistinct, yet stirring and working presentiment, that all the products of the mere reflective faculty partook of death* (*BL*, Ch. IX, pp. 69–70). The metaphysical map opposite may help you to navigate your imagination through the strange journey of one man's soul, his experience of good and evil and his safe home-coming by the grace of God and nature.

Part I

2 **he stoppeth one of three**   The Mariner chooses the man who is the closest blood relation to the bridegroom and therefore the chief guest, cutting right across the bonds and duties of family life.

3, 17 **glittering eye**   suggests mania and hypnosis. Cf. with Coleridge's reference to the bright eyes of his son by moonlight and those of the nightingales, lines 67 and 104 in *The Nightingale*.

5 **The Bridegroom**   in theological terms, Christ himself. Remember that during the telling of the Mariner's tale a wedding ceremony is taking place.

13 **skinny hand**   The Mariner is thin as a beggar, one who can find no rest in earthly life. He has been compared with the Wandering Jew, who rejected Christ and was condemned to earthly immortality.

28 **the Light-house top**   is a symbol of that which saves mariners from dangerous rocks – the last thing he sees of home and the first on his return (see line 470).

29 As the ship sails south, the rising sun is seen on the left, or

the Ideal East, and sets on the right, or the Ideal West. Everything is normal. We are not told the destination of the ship, nor its name. We never learn if there is a captain, nor what rank the Mariner holds.

34 The ship reaches the Equator, a vital point in the Mariner's story, but is interrupted by the Wedding Guest's realization that the bride has entered the church. What relationship can you see between these two events?

41 **he beat his breast** he is distraught but *cannot chuse but hear.*

47–48 Having reached the Equator – the crossing point of the four poles – a fierce storm strikes the ship. Powerless, it is driven southwards towards the Antarctic. This *land of mist and snow* is a world of suspended animation (Coleridge uses the word *ice* six times in the next few verses), a lifeless world of crystals – *As green as Emerauld* – yet still beautiful. There are echoes of Dante's *Inferno* here.

51 **Ice mast-high** The symbol of the cross-like mast represents that elevating principle which resists death.

55 There is no sentient life, only the force of Repulsion or Alienation.

59–60 **swound** is a swoon or faint. This world may symbolize the unconscious life of the mind. The noises seem elemental – the polar opposites of that warm-blooded humanity seen in the bride – *red as a rose.*

61 At one level this white and innocent creature is nature's benign force, sent to rescue those who have trespassed into alien territory. At another it is seen as a Christ-like redeemer. The Mariner hails it as *a Christian Soul* (line 63) and *in God's name* (line 64). All Coleridge's poems in *Lyrical Ballads* mention birds. A beautiful note on line 74 of his poem *This Lime Tree Bower my Prison* might apply to the flight of the albatross:

The birds move their wings in flight, their strokes are slow, moderate and regular; and even when at a considerable distance or high above us, we plainly hear the quill-feathers: their shafts and webs upon one another creek as the joints or working of a vessel in a tempestuous sea.

(*The Poems of Samuel Taylor Coleridge*, ed. E.H. Coleridge, Oxford University Press, 1912, p. 184)

65 **biscuit-worms** feeding the albatross with alien food.

67 Magically, the sterile powers of an alien land are challenged by the power of Repulsion. The ship is freed and death challenged. Internal rhyme is a style to be used throughout the poem.

73–74 The bird appears like a holy spirit attending evening prayers. Moonlight – associated with Christ – was a sacred time for Coleridge.

77–78 The Wedding Guest re-enters the narrative at the precise point at which the Mariner re-lives his crime. He is shocked to witness the Mariner's agony as he seems tormented by fiends. Significantly, the weapon is a crossbow. The murder cuts across the laws of hospitality, the sailors seeming ungrateful guests betraying their host's good will. Consider the Mariner's motives for this cruel act – sadistic pleasure, the need to impress his shipmates, malice, perversity, a sense of social exclusion, or was it an unfeeling act caused by mere thoughtlessness? Whatever the reason, the life of the spirit is rejected. The sailors are plunged into a world of their lower senses. Not until they return to the Equator – that area unprotected by nature's benign influence – do they recognize what a consuming fire of damnation they have unleashed.

Part II

81 The ship is driven back upon its former path, so the pattern of sunrise and sunset appears reversed. All seems normal.

89 The reference to hell raises the subject of damnation. At first angered by the Mariner's cruel act, the sailors then agree with it and in their moral confusion partake in his guilt. The Sun – an image of Christ's resurrection and mediating power – rises gloriously. The wind – the sailors' blessing – blows strongly. The ship hastens joyfully towards its damnation.

101–102 **burst** implies a kind of explosive entry into some totally strange medium. The **silent sea** is no ordinary place. The poem enters the supernatural. Everything that occurs in this void is dreamlike and unreal.

104 Sadness is the first emotion referred to in this place, and it is one to which Coleridge returns. The mood suggests a feeling

of being abandoned by God. Of melancholia Coleridge has much to say. In a notebook of the period he writes: *Melancholy is like an earthquake to one in a dungeon, which for a small moment makes the very walls gape and cleave and so lets in light for a while at those chinks; but all closes up again, and leaves the Prisoner to his wonted Darkness (Notebooks,* vol. I, Text 1000I). Compare this state of misery with that in *The Dungeon* and *The Convict*.)

108 At the Equator – the crossing point of the four poles – the sun appears not glorious but *bloody*, symbolic of the crucified Christ. Bereft now of nature's protection and having alienated the divine being (God – or the spiritual in man), the sailors are at the mercy of their own base natures – original sin (that into which mankind fell after the transgression of Adam). Seen through their diseased imaginations the sun is just a ball of fire. Heat and thirst ensue. The Mariner's loneliness is caused by the suspension of ordinary time. A passage in *BL* helps us to understand this

...the two poles of the magnet manifest the being and unity of the one power by relative opposites, and give as it were, a substratum of permanence, of identity, and therefore of reality, to the shadowy flux of time...The Mystics have joined in representing the state of the reprobate spirits as a dreadful dream in which there is no sense of reality.

(*Biographia Literaria*, ed. J. Shawcross, 2 vols, Clarendon Press, 1907, vol. II, pp. 207–8)

113–114 Everything changes from being three-dimensional to two-dimensional. Movement ceases, because all that flows is the essence of life. Here is a vacuum in which things are silent and sterile. No one speaks, each locked in his own dungeon of the self.

117–118 Surrounded by God's bounty, man is barren; without a wind, the ship is helpless.

119–122 Corruption seems the product of a fevered mind (possibly elements of Coleridge's opium dreams) but also a heightened sense of the incredibility of corruption as seen through the more noble senses.

123–126 Coleridge had read of the translucent colours of tropical
fish. List the colours mentioned in this poem. Seen by
moonlight, even the rotting sea partakes of God's abundant
beauty. These creatures seem trapped in physical matter but
are magical, supernatural. In a later epigraph to the poem
Coleridge quotes from Thomas Burnett: *There are as many
invisible orders of angels as there are fish in the sea.*

137–138 Guilt is transferred to the Mariner, absolving the sailors from
those purgatorial experiences, or suffering designed to
expiate sin which he must suffer, and thus leaving them free
to die. The Mariner becomes a marked man.

Part III

139–148 Exactly at the time when the setting sun is about to pass over
the horizon and the moon and stars are hidden, the skeleton
ship approaches. Its movement – *It plung'd and tack'd and
veer'd* – is awkward, as if coping with a foreign element.

152–153 For both poets the word *blood* has deep significance. Here the
shedding of blood, an act of self-sacrifice (one would say
now, an act of self-harming) brings partial release. A flash of
joy allows a symbolic drinking by the sailors.

163, 167–169 These beautiful images of burning have resonance beyond the
poem. Coleridge felt his imagination to be most active when
dreaming beside a fireside.

171–172 This conveys a nightmare quality beyond ordinary reality.
(Cf. images of suffering in *The Dungeon*.)

177 **Are these *her* naked ribs** In a later version Coleridge added
A bare Anatomy, a clue to the original meaning. The ship
represents the base material lacking God's creative spirit.

181–189 Death is a skeleton vivid with the hectic colours of the grave.
Death in Life is an incarnation of lust; a whore (in
Revelations, The Whore of Babylon) characterized by garish
colours. She epitomizes disease; those sensual parts of man
that degrade. The couple seem as man and wife, or Adam and
Eve, an appalling association with the marriage ceremony
being celebrated during the telling of the tale. Adam and Eve
are the eternal opposites of male and female by which life is
created and God manifests his nature in the world. In the

following verse we learn that the two are dicing for the Mariner's soul. Death in Life wins. Thus Death takes the souls of the other mariners. Why should the Mariner's soul be worth all the rest?

190 **Her flesh makes the air cold** later changed to *Who thicks man's blood with cold*. Fear was a sense much studied by both poets for it is something in the mind that affects the body. Coleridge believed fear to be an essentially non-human emotion, supernatural and illusory. Thus evil is the greatest lie against the spirit.

195 There is a custom in folklore that witches can conjure winds. A more likely explanation is that nature rushes to protect her own. As the moon rises the ghostly ship darts away. The moon is *horned...with one bright Star* (line 202) – the star being a daemonic influence – and Death claims the sailors. Two hundred men die, each cursing the Mariner and recalling his experience of killing the Albatross.

Part IV

216 The Wedding Guest thinks he may be seeing a phantom. The word *fear* is mentioned five times in the next seven lines – an emotion to be described again in lines 451–456 as a sense of being pursued by *a dreadful fiend*. But what *is* fear? Which of the following do you think most nearly describes the emotion? Nature's defence mechanism, a sudden withdrawal of nature's or God's protective spirit, a kind of bewitching spell (whose effects are pallor, trembling, loss of bodily control, being rooted to the spot, running away), or an evil visitation?

218–219 This snake-like image was suggested by Wordsworth.

223 Like Macbeth, the Mariner bears a charmed life, even when the ship sinks, as one *seven days drown'd/My body lay afloat* (lines 582–583).

224–227 This is the state of being entirely without God. The soul seems withered and the universe empty of meaning.

230–231 The Mariner wishes he too could have died. He equates himself with the slimy creatures of the deep, daemons trapped in physical matter.

232–254 These two stanzas dramatically describe a kind of

crucifixion. The Mariner seems symbolically stretched across
the four poles and the four elements. Nothing can relieve his
agony, and he longs to die. Like Macbeth after the murder of
Duncan, he cannot pray.

255–260 A moving description of the star-filled heavens. The contrast
between the cold light of the moon and the red corrupting
sea emphasizes the polarity between heaven and hell, frost
and fire. The *charm'd water* seems to burn. A notebook entry
of the period quotes Boehme: *That all is God's self – that a
man's self is God if he live holily – that the Waters of this world
are mad* (*Notebooks*, vol. I, Text 1000E).

We now approach the turning point of the whole poem – the
Blessing of the Water Snakes (Coleridge does not call them
fish). The idea of the serpent appears in Boehme as a symbol of
unenlightened materialism. The water snakes' elfish and
phosphorescent beauty, their movement like flashing fire, make
the Mariner forget his own torment. By moonlight (Christ) he is
privileged to see the harmony that created the universe. The
word *flash* in line 273 is significant, as it is for Wordsworth as an
opening of the inner vision. However, Wordsworth's *flashing* in
the *inner eye* is different from Coleridge's, which is essentially a
transcendental experience. The Mariner is privileged to receive a
vision of the supernatural. In the context of the poem we may
compare this *flashing* with the beams of the lighthouse and those
different manifestations of glittering light in this and other
poems. It also has alchemical associations connected to
magnetism and early notions of electricity. (Mary Shelley uses
electricity as the source of creation in *Frankenstein*.)

276–277 Love is symbolized by the sentient element of spring water.
This describes the elevating principle that is opposed to all
those things in the poem that are flat, heavy and dead. The
blessing is *unaware*, given by grace alone. Blessing is a two-
fold act, conveying God's blessing on another yet invoking
spiritual protection for oneself: as Wordsworth exclaims in
Lines Written a Few Miles above Tintern Abbey, all which we

behold/*Is full of blessings* (lines 134–135); and Coleridge writes
in a letter of 1802, *everything has a life of its own, and that we
are all one life* (*Letters*, vol. II, p. 864). Prayer opens the
channels of forgiveness. To shoot the Albatross had been to
violate the harmony of the universe. Now it falls *like lead*
into the sea. This shedding of the corpse of the Albatross is
the prelude to further visions of the ideal universe.

Part V

284–300 The sense of time becomes fluid. The Mariner's inner eye is
opened. In sleep, his body rests like a child in its mother's
arms and his soul drinks from the invisible world. This is a
state between life and death – as all sleep may be. In fact, in
line 299, the Mariner believes that he has died. Forces
previously hidden now become visible. Life returns to the
ship first as a roaring wind, then in heavy rain.

305–338 Under the influence of the third phase of the moon the dead
sailors' bodies are inhabited by angelic spirits. As a limb
deprived of blood seems a lifeless tool, so the bodies have no
human identity. The Mariner's nephew works the ropes next
to him but does not recognize him. At dawn the spirits
return to the sun from which they have come. What follows
next is a passage of the deepest mysticism.

339–346 The idea that sound and light are related is an idea Coleridge
may have taken from a number of sources, possibly from
Dante but probably from Boehme's *Aurora*. A reference to
this is found in a letter of 1817, the idea that *Sound was =
Light under the praepotence of Gravitation, and Color =
Gravitation under the praepotence of Light* (*Letters*, vol. IV,
p. 751). Boehme's own reflection helps us with this idea. *First
there is the* Power, *and in the Power is the Tone or* Tune, *which
rises up in the Spirit, into the Head, into the* Mind...*and in the
Mind it has its* Seat...*For the Fountain of all Powers floweth in
the Heart* (quoted in J.B. Beer, *Coleridge the Visionary*, Chatto
& Windus, 1959, p. 62). For Coleridge, heart and mind in
union can alone perceive the lost Paradise. The song of the
lark – a glimpse of the divine – blended with heavenly music,
symbolizes universal harmony (the music of the spheres).

In Hermetic philosophy the individual life of each creature has its own tone. The noise of falling water mentioned in line 358 is suggestive of a kind of heavenly bliss (see Henry Vaughan, *The Waterfall*).

364–365 These lines suggest the power of animal magnetism or hypnosis.

366 The word *sad* used three times in the next three lines refers us to that *silent sea*, a sadness born out of exclusion. Notice that the Mariner seems unable to speak with his shipmates. They seem to see *through* him as if he is *thin as air* (line 376). This raises again the question of why the Mariner is so different from the others.

384 **The spirit slid** the Spirit of the South Pole or Repulsion. In line 368 we are told that the sun is still above the mast at noon. In spite of its apparent motion, the ship has not moved. A battle takes place between light and heat and the power of Repulsion. The Polar Spirit prevails and, with a sudden bound, the ship is partly freed from the spell. The Mariner falls into a trance in which he hears two angelic voices, the first telling him that the lonely Spirit of the South Pole who loved the Albatross requires further vengeance, and the other promising that this will take place.

Part VI

The image of the sea staring heavenwards as some huge, bright, open eye is one of those stunning metaphors which seem to come from the Secondary Imagination (see Interpretations, p. 198). The second angel informs the first that 'The air is cut away before/And closes from behind' (lines 429–430). This curious form of locomotion may be explained by recalling that the focus of the four poles at which most of the action takes place is a void or vacuum. The effects of wind are nullified and a more direct remedy sought. Only while the Mariner is entranced can divine spirits intercede.

435 The Mariner wakes. It is a calm, moonlit night. The men stand together, their eyes glittering, seeming to curse the Mariner.

447 The spell is broken.

457–488 The ship is again introduced to the world of nature and a sweet breeze reminiscent of spring carries it homewards. *But soon there breath'd a wind on me.* The word *breath* is significant since God is the *breath of life.* The act of *breathing* – also used frequently by Wordsworth – employs the forces of expansion and contraction. The first thing the Mariner sees is the top of the lighthouse, then the rock on which stands the church. Home seems a more blessed place than he had ever imagined, but there is none of that *merry* mood with which he left. Instead, his soul feels wonder and exaltation, suggested by the moonlight which floods the bay and an uncanny stillness – another example of Coleridge's use of image to create a mood rather than stated thought. This prepares us for an astonishing vision.

490 The word *rood* is an old English word meaning the cross. The sailors stand at its foot, each holding his right arm upright which burns like a torch. One interpretation may be that by his suffering the Mariner is privileged to see that intense light – the Hand of Glory – by which each human soul comes into the world and leaves it (in Buddhism this is called *Atma* or *Spirit Man*). In alarm the Mariner turns his eyes away only to see the church standing upon the rock. When he looks again at the deck, an angel stands upon each corpse. This time, light and sound are not associated, but the silence is *like music on my heart* (line 526). The word *heart* is used three times in the poem, each time with the sense that it is the living centre of humanity distinct from *soul*; a human rather than a divine entity. (See Note to lines 339–346.)

527–544 The Pilot, his boy and the Hermit have seen the *signals.*

545–546 The Mariner's first thought on coming home is to seek confession – to be *shrieved* – and forgiveness. (See the illustration opposite.) Part VI ends on the word *blood*, a word that is rhymed in the first line of Part VII. *Blood* is a word much used in *Lyrical Ballads* but Wordsworth and Coleridge understood very different things by it. Here it has a religious connotation preparing us for a major theme in the final part – the nature of prayer and salvation through Christ.

'*Oh shrieve me, shrieve me, holy man!*' *The Ancient Mariner* by Gustave
Doré. (Image: © Archivo Iconografico, S.A./CORBIS)

Part VII

The Hermit is, like the Wedding Guest, an important figure, and is a man of prayer and imagination whose life is simple and close to nature. Coleridge mentions three symbols in connection with him – the brook, the wolf and the owl, all of which appear in other poems in *Lyrical Ballads*. That the owls devour the offspring of the wolf perhaps implies nature's rapacious cycle of birth and death. Coleridge associated himself with the owl.

582 **The ship went down like lead**   as does the corpse of the Albatross.

585–586 Seven is a magical number in religion, myth and folk-lore.

611–623 The next three stanzas deal with the Mariner's guilt. Confession is painful, causing *woeful agony* (line 612). Each time he repeats his tale the cycle of the betrayal of Christ and his crucifixion is repeated, as indeed it is in the continued sins of the world. Speaking of this Coleridge wrote in 1817: *the whole process is cyclical tho' progressive* (*Notebooks*, vol. IV, p. 769).

624 Do you remember Coleridge's previous use of the word *burst* in line 101? Here, warm human life returns as the guests stream out of church to attend the bridal feast.

The final stanzas, some of which were regretted by Coleridge (though interestingly, he kept them in his final version), deal with the subject of prayer and moral truth. We may summarize them as:

- Prayer and love are inseparable. The goal of the mystic is not mere knowledge of the supernatural but union with it through love.
- Creation is formed from divine love.
- Communal acts of worship are as essential as private prayer.
- All sentient life is sacred.
- Suffering is a necessary precondition to human wisdom.

These are just a few of the moral values that emerge in the poem. You may wish to consider others.

651–653 The Mariner disappears almost as quickly as he had appeared. Though there is still time to join the celebration, the Wedding Guest turns away *stunn'd* and *forlorn* having been offered richer spiritual food.

657–658 What sad things did the Wedding Guest learn? Why should sadness accompany wisdom? (See Keats's comment on *Lines Written a Few Miles above Tintern Abbey* in Notes, pp. 175–6).

In a *Notebook* entry Coleridge's comments: *It is not true that men always go gradually from good to evil and evil to good. Sometimes a flash of lightning will turn the magnetic poles* (*Notebooks*, vol. I, p. 432, f. 53.29). What flash of lightning changed the Mariner? Is he drawn naturalistically or symbolically? How old do you think he is? Is he a tragic hero, a madman, a good storyteller, or just a garrulous old fool like the sea captain in *The Thorn*? Do you have sympathy for him? In the time scheme of his story he endures much, but suffers in silence, and only when he returns home is his tongue loosed. What obsession drives him? Compare him with another storyteller in *Lyrical Ballads*.

Although Coleridge drew on his copious reading, the result is a work of staggering originality and imagination. He was to wonder himself at the creative processes which had brought it to birth and his theory of the imagination is, to some extent, based on it. Why do you think it is seen as a masterpiece which is greater than the mere sum of its parts? Read the poem a number of times. Only when you are familiar with the way that metre, sound, rhythm and imagery are an organic unity will you understand Coleridge's wonderful achievement.

The Foster-Mother's Tale

Three out of four of Coleridge's poems are in blank verse, or unrhymed lines in iambic pentameter, having ten syllables in the line – a form in which he was most at ease. This extract is from Act IV of Coleridge's play *Osorio* (1797), later entitled *Remorse*. Albert, presumed murdered by his brother Osorio, returns to his family home disguised as a conjuror and arranges to meet his beloved Maria at their foster-mother's cottage. He is arrested for sorcery and thrown into one of his father's dungeons where, in Act V, he speaks the soliloquy presented as *The Dungeon* in *Lyrical Ballads*. The foster-mother tells the story of a youth whom she knew in childhood. Stories of foundling children are well established in fiction, and works as diverse as *Oedipus Rex* and *Babes in the Wood* draw upon these touching human tales. Coleridge expresses serious views on the education of children. Many of the poems in *Lyrical Ballads* explore the theme of motherhood as the deepest, most sacred of human emotions.

24 **mosses, lined** Moss is associated with the baby's grave in *The Thorn*. These verbal links are evidence that the poets discussed each other's work.

31 Coleridge considered birdsong as embryonic poetry. Hazlitt records Coleridge reading Wordsworth's ballads to him in 1798 and talking expertly on the song of the nightingale. Coleridge also discussed nightingales with Keats in 1819, shortly after which Keats was to write his famous ode. As a child, Wordsworth enjoyed imitating birds' songs, delighting in fooling them into replying. It is significant that many of the poems in *Lyrical Ballads* include references to birds. The subject figures widely in Romantic literature.

36 **simples** medicinal plants.

41 **a very learned youth** Intellectually gifted and an obsessive reader as a boy, Coleridge once ran away from home, stayed out all night and slept beside the river Otter, catching a serious fever. The boy's delirium is another example of the many references in *Lyrical Ballads* to disturbed states of mind.

57 **cast into that hole**   A common punishment at Christ's
   Hospital was being locked up for the night in a cupboard.
   Coleridge condemned all physical violence against children.

63 The reference to a naked man may allude to Jean-Jacques
   Rousseau's concept of *the naked savage*. Rousseau's *Emile*
   (1762), a work on the education of children, was influential
   in furthering the idea of greater liberty for the individual.
   The reference to the *savannah* touches on Coleridge's
   Pantisocratic theory.

81 **he lived and died among the savage men**   Consider the
   foster-mother's final view. Does the boy find the freedom he
   longs for in line 64, or is his end – in her eyes – tragic?

Lines left upon a Seat in a Yew-tree, which stands near the Lake of Esthwaite

This is the first of Wordsworth's poems in the collection and it is
also in blank verse. It is interesting in that it describes a man
withdrawn from the world because of disappointed ambitions.
Wordsworth's epic poem *The Recluse* – a grandiose scheme
proposed by Coleridge, at which he would labour for the next four
decades – would never achieve the philosophic stature to which its
author aspired. Most of his poetry is preoccupied with solitude
and withdrawal from a world of increasing industrialization and
social change. The long sub-title is used in many of the poems and
was common in poetry magazines of the 1790s. The *Gentleman's
Magazine* of the period abounds in ballads about the poor, the
abandoned, the criminal and the insane (see Robert Mayo, 'The
contemporaneity of Lyrical Ballads', *Publications of the Modern
Language Association of America*, vol. xix, 1954, pp. 486–522). The
exactness with which Wordsworth locates the place – in the Lake
District – lends weight to the idea that this is another of his
boyhood retreats. The builder of the seat was a fellow pupil but his
misanthropy is an invention.

1 **Nay Traveller! rest** This direct address, later becoming *Stranger* and *Thou seest*, immediately establishes a relationship with someone out walking. This was a time when tourists were visiting the Lake District attracted by guides to picturesque landscapes composed by writers such as William Gilpin, whose book *Observations on the River Wye* (1782) accompanied the Wordsworths on their tour of the Wye Valley in 1798. The address also makes the place particular.

4 Yew trees are associated with graveyards and death. Words such as *lonely, gloomy* and *barren* define a forsaken spot.

7 **vacancy** a depressing emptiness. (Cf. *in vacant or in pensive mood* in his poem '*I wandered lonely as a Cloud*'.)

8–9 **who he was/That piled these stones** Wordsworth was interested in how we impose our identity on abstract things – an idea to be explored fully in his poem *Michael*.

11 **to bend its arms in circling shade** the human impulse to deform or destroy growing things.

18 **All but neglect** suggests his spirit languished because his work was neglected. A highly ambitious man himself, Wordsworth was interested in worldly failure. Through solitude this man sustains his sense of identity.

23–26 Nature does not desert him. Sheep, birds and the changing seasons are his companions.

27 **Fixing his downward eye** an image of a man lost in sad reflections. Does this imply self-pity?

30–34 These lines raise the theme of beauty as consolation. Wordsworth's word *beauteous* is used in *The Thorn* and elsewhere. How does it differ from *beautiful*? Another favourite word is *gaze – I gazed and gazed* in '*I wandered lonely as a Cloud*'.

43 **this seat his only monument** stresses the brief nature of human life compared with the vastness of time. The final section rebukes human pride and self-absorption. True dignity resides with the man who retains love and humility.

Blank verse was a medium in which Wordsworth would excel. Though the subject is Romantic, there are several touches of eighteenth-century grandeur. Line 3, *No sparkling rivulet spread the verdant herb*, has an almost Augustan artificiality. The didactic tone *O, be wiser thou!* (line 55) shows him keen to convey moral values in the manner of John Milton. Consider why both Wordsworth and Coleridge chose blank verse for their more personal poems?

The Nightingale

Wordsworth's poem on melancholy is closely followed by Coleridge's poem on what is traditionally a melancholy bird. His footnote to line 13 qualifies Milton's line *most musical, most melancholy* (from *Il Penseroso*, line 62), though he restricts the description to the character of those who have described it, not to the bird itself. Coleridge was initiating a tradition. The poem has all the ingredients of romance – those *melodies of woods, and winds, and waters* referred to in line 24 of *The Dungeon*. The scene is bathed in moonlight and contains everything the true Romantic adores: gentle damsels, medieval ruins, books, birds, secret dells and things *half hidden from the eye* (for what the eye cannot see must be imagined).

The poem was completed on 10 May 1798 and the setting is the landscape near Alfoxden (see the illustration on page 7). It is sub-titled *A Conversational Poem*. There are others written at this time which you may like to read (*This Lime Tree Bower my Prison* and *Frost at Midnight*) which, like this poem, capture the tone and articulation of Coleridge's voice. Even the punctuation here is worth close study, the question and exclamation marks suggesting someone in the very act of thinking and feeling. This immediacy of thought contrasting with Wordsworth's *emotion recollected in tranquillity* was a quality to be much emulated by later Romantics. Coleridge's emotions are anything *but* tranquil. The poem is dynamic and vivacious, as if he is directly engaged with the life of nature.

Notes

1   **relique**   remains.

7   **verdure**   moss.

9   **vernal**   spring-like.

13–23   Coleridge attributes a jaundiced view of the bird to earlier poets who had projected their own sadness onto nature. This was exactly what later Romantics would do. Pathetic fallacy, or attributing to nature human emotions, was to characterize much literature of the later nineteenth century. Coleridge's debt to Milton, like Wordsworth's, is extensive. There are copious echoes of Book IV of *Paradise Lost* and *the wakeful nightingale*.

23   **conceit**   a contrived figure of speech usually implying a contradiction.

25–34   Although Coleridge was more concerned with the *making* of poetry than Wordsworth, he advises the poet not to slave over his composition but to experience nature directly. At this stage, Coleridge might have been in accord with the view in *The Tables Turned* that *One impulse from a vernal wood* (line 21) teaches us about the soul of man, but he would hold that nature can say little about morality.

39   **Philomela's pity-pleading strains**   The reference is from Ovid's *Metamorphosis*, Book VI, pages 425ff. Tereus, king of Thrace, has ravished his sister-in-law Philomela. To prevent her from revealing her story, her tongue is cut out. After her martyrdom, she is turned into a nightingale.

40   **My Friend, and my Friend's Sister**   Wordsworth and Dorothy. It is interesting that neither poet ever refers to Dorothy by name in any of his poems.

48–49   **disburthen his full soul/Of all its music!**   The section beginning *I know a grove* (line 49) has a tone of secrecy shared with the reader. The exuberance of the song is beautifully captured.

54–55   The repetition of the word *grass – and grass/Thin grass –* conveys the poet searching for the perfect descriptive word so anxious is he to be precise, yet so caught up in wonder and excitement. There is a sudden surge of alliteration and onamatopoeia in lines 59–61:

> With skirmish and capricious passagings,
> And murmers musical and swift jug jug
> And one low piping sound more sweet than all –

This suggests that the bird is an artist.

64–69 The repetition of *bright* (line 67) calls up thoughts of the
       Mariner's *glittering eye*. Moonlight is a stimulus to song – an
       idea apparently correct in ornithology. The glow-worm's
       answering *love-torch* depicts a harmony in nature (see line 62)
       while expanding the fairy beauty of the scene. For another
       description of this *breeze* of nature, see Wordsworth's
       I Heard a Thousand Blended Notes.
   65 **dewy leafits**   half-opened leaves.
   69 **a most gentle maid**   The lines following refer not to
       Dorothy but to Ellen Cruikshank, whose father was the Earl
       of Egmont.
84–86 The springing rhythm is in tune with the bird's joyous music.
   86 **tipsy Joy**   a phrase from Milton's *L'Allegro.*

The final paragraph describes a farewell to friends and introduces
the subject of childhood. Coleridge was determined that his own
son Hartley (1796–1849) would not suffer the unhappiness which
he had experienced at Christ's Hospital. His sentiments on
childhood reflect something of Rousseau's view that each child
should be free to develop its own innate character while living as
close as possible to the influences of nature. This is a fond
father's memory, especially poignant because Hartley would lose
his fellowship at Oxford and later take to drink. Though he
wrote some poetry, he led a troubled and lonely life.

104–105 Both poets were interested in the images associated with eyes.
         There are 19 references to *eyes* in *The Rime of the Ancyent
         Marinere*!

You will have noticed that the styles of these two poets differ
even when using the same form. Each has found a style

particularly suited to his character: Coleridge's enthusiastic and intellectually energetic; Wordsworth's calm, reflective and possibly more introverted.

The Female Vagrant

Composed between 1793 and 1794, this is an extract from the narrative poem *Guilt and Sorrow* – said to be a true story of a soldier's widow and her voyage home from America. For Wordsworth, this was a period of foreboding about the outcome of the war with France. Vagrants play a prominent part in his poetry (see *The Old Cumberland Beggar* and *The Leech Gatherer*). This was a time when the state was reducing alms' giving to the poor. Wordsworth saw in these solitaries a power of endurance and a wise passiveness. The literary critic John Jones calls these figures *gatherers up of time* (*The Egotistical Sublime*, Chatto & Windus, 1954, p. 67), timeless, almost primordial beings who have acquired stillness and mystery. Compare the Ancient Mariner with Wordsworth's wanderers, considering which acquire serenity and which remain troubled.

The poem is written in Spenserian stanzas: an iambic line close to ordinary speech but formalized by a strict rhyme scheme. The narrative is a chronicle of events beginning with a kind of family paradise of independence, piety and hard work. Nature smiles on the father's small farm until it is lost to a rich landowner. There follows decline, madness and despair. There are distinct echoes in language and sentiment of Thomas Gray's *Elegy Written in a Country Churchyard*.

> 8 **fleecy store** a flock of sheep – a very eighteenth-century figure of speech. Others include *May's dewy prime* (line 25), *snowy pride* (line 27), *wild brood* (line 215), *milky udder* (line 225) and *jocund June* (line 233).

36 **The red-breast known for years**   Living close to nature, the family feed the wild birds, sharing their good fortune.

39 **Then rose a mansion proud**   This marks an ominous moment when what Gray calls *The little Tyrant of his Fields* swallows both the father's living and the family's security. Unlike Godwin, Wordsworth defended hereditary property.

51 **his little range of water**   This withdrawal seems the ultimate treachery.

53 **All, all was seized.**   The Enclosure Acts of 1803–1816 were soon to foreclose on smallholders, driving farm labourers to the cities where they would became dependent on the uncertainties of capital and exposed to the greed of factory owners. A poet affected by this Act was John Clare, the Northamptonshire poet greatly influenced by Wordsworth. Clare's removal from his native home drove him to insanity.

59–60 Canon law still upholds the right for a person to be buried in his native place. Uprooting the family is the main cause of the woman's tragedy.

89 **The empty loom, cold hearth and silent wheel**   are the effects of the collapse of the cottage industry. Although poorly paid, such work guaranteed a degree of independence.

93–94 **the noisy drum/Beat round**   the press gang. There were only two choices for the destitute: flight to the industrial towns or enlistment in the army to fight for England in the American War of Independence. Some families who joined their menfolk on troop ships died of famine, shipwreck or disease. These are all acts of nature conflicting with Wordsworth's belief that nature does not betray those who love her.

154–162 This stanza refers to the fire, murder and rape in which the female vagrant's sanity gives way, a hell created by man. Nature's *balmy air* brings to her a kind of blessing.

235–243 Begging is at first an indignity until hunger makes it a necessity. She receives common kindness from a band of gipsies. Thieving is alien to her upbringing. Finally, she takes to the highway alone.

258–259 Her soul feels the sharpest pain from moral decline (see *The Last of the Flock*) and the poem ends in despair. In his *Preface* Wordsworth defines poetry as emotion *recollected in tranquillity*, but here suffering remains unrelieved by time.

Almost the entire poem consists of the woman's own words. Is this *the real language of men*? How *artless* (line 2) is her story? How far is she a credible human being? Of all Wordsworth's female figures, only Goody Blake rebels against her fate, though three women find relief in maternal love. This poem was to be much copied by later poets. One of the most highly regarded ballads in English in this style is Thomas Hardy's *A Tramp Woman's Tragedy*.

Goody Blake and Harry Gill

Written at Alfoxden in 1798 and referred to in the Advertisement as a true story, Wordsworth clearly felt affection for this poem. In the Preface he tells us:

> I wished to draw attention to the truth that the power of the human imagination is sufficient to produce such changes even in our own physical nature as might almost appear miraculous.

(Appendices, p. 240)

Several of Wordsworth's poems are concerned with disturbed mental states, and he was familiar with Erasmus Darwin's *Zoonomia, or the Laws of Organic Life* (1796), which describes a state of *mania mutabilis* in which the imagination produces what we now describe as psychosomatic illness.

The poem's structure is unusual: an eight-line stanza with alternate rhymes and a pattern of seven, eight and nine syllabic lines, though not entirely consistent. This creates a brisk tempo suitable for the telling of a homely and slightly comic tale. The tone is uncertain – possibly the reason why it has been much maligned. Sympathy is clearly with Goody Blake and those denied their common human rights.

17 **lusty drover** Harry is a healthy young shepherd; Goody is old and ill fed.

25 **All day she spun** cottage industry wages were meagre.

39 **canty** bright and cheerful. Winter could be fatal to the old.

Verse 7 The lively metre imitates the boisterous wind. Storms were useful to Goody because they saved her the labour of cutting sticks.

Verse 8 An old hedge was easy picking for her since it would be dry and good for burning. A sensible farmer might have welcomed Goody's action since it removed the dead wood and encouraged new growth.

65 **long suspected** This shows Harry's pettiness. His creeping stealthily down the hill makes him a ludicrous figure. His waiting until she fills her apron is malicious.

97–99 Her curse, *her wither'd hand uprearing*, is a dramatic moment and takes effect almost at once. Here is that supernatural power in ordinary things.

124–128 The last verse dwells on Harry's fate: a warning to those who ignore scriptural teaching on charity in the distribution of the fruits of nature.

Lines, Written at a Small Distance from my House

The long sub-title was changed in 1845 to *To my Sister*. The little boy was the son of Basil Montagu, a mutual friend through whom Wordsworth and Coleridge were to quarrel in 1810, and finally part. Wordsworth revisited Alfoxden in 1841 and noticed that the larch mentioned in line 3 was still alive. The poem is written in identical form to *Lines Written in Early Spring* and achieves a simplicity and naturalness of expression appropriate to the theme.

12 **Come forth and feel the sun** Wordsworth delighted in sharing experiences with his sister. Her notebooks were an invaluable aid to his composition. (See Sandra Anstey's

useful notes on this aspect of Wordsworth's work in the
Oxford Student Texts edition of *William Wordsworth: Selected
Poems*, 2006, pp. 8–10.)

Verse 6 The sun's rays seem to radiate love *from heart to heart* (line
22). Here is an example of Wordsworth's pantheism. All
sentient life is connected *To her fair works did nature link/The
human soul that through me ran* (*Lines Written in Early Spring*,
lines 5–6; see this poem for a further example of this
continuity from nature to man).

25–26 Wordsworth's faith in emotion and intuition far outweigh his
trust in intellect. Wordsworth suggests that wisdom can almost
be imbibed through the air. He equates *mind* and *pore*, as if the
intellect can breathe a *blessed power* (line 33). This is that

motion and a spirit, that impels
All thinking things, all objects of all thought
And rolls through all things.

in *Tintern Abbey* (lines 101–102). What is this spirit that rolls
About, below, above in line 34 – a grasping for a sublime
oneness with creation, a religious faith, a deistic system of
explaining the universe, or merely what Coleridge called
mental bombast?

40 **idleness**   As a result of an annuity granted to him by his
friend Raisley Calvert, Wordsworth was fortunate in being
able to lead a gentleman's life. Though his wants were few, he
did not need to earn a living, unlike Coleridge. He believed
that idleness was essential both to artistic and spiritual life.
How does this view bear on Wordsworth's attitude to the
labouring poor?

Simon Lee, the Old Huntsman

Simon Lee had been huntsman to the squires of Alfoxden.
Wordsworth transfers the location to Cardiganshire, perhaps to
avoid upsetting the local gentry. There is an implied criticism of

those who use the loyal services of the poor only to abandon them to destitution in old age. The words *He dearly loves their voices* (line 48) are said to be Simon's own – words from common speech, which have a poetic ring.

9–10, 12 It is difficult to make sense of these lines. Can his coat be fair before but *not* behind? How do we know *at once* that he is poor? Line 15 also seems odd.

Verse 5 describes Simon's decrepitude. The reference to his swollen ankles here and again in line 68 are examples of Wordsworth's tendency to include exact details taken from actual life. He is anxious to record a true picture and impress upon us that an old, sick man should not have to do manual labour after he has spent his life serving the rich and privileged.

60 The sad irony is that Simon and Ruth, now frail, are unable to tend the small amount of land it has take them a lifetime to enclose.

Verse 13 Wordsworth delivers the moral lesson when Simon bursts into tears. He has asked for so little yet displays such gratitude. Wordsworth was opposed to Godwin's theory that gratitude is a degrading emotion born out of inequality.

Do you think that the poem is flawed or should we see it as part of the experimental nature of *Lyrical Ballads*? Certainly it shows the problem of trying to be too literal. Coleridge questioned whether Wordsworth had ever used truly natural speech. In Chapter XVIII of *Biographia Literaria*, Coleridge claims that the language of *The Sailor's Mother* is *the only fair instance that I have been able to discover in all Mr. Wordsworth's writings of an actual adoption, or true imitation, of the real...language of low and rustic life, freed from provincialisms* (*BL*, Ch. XVIII, p. 181).

Anecdote for Fathers

This poem was also composed in 1798. The boy was the son of Basil Montagu. Wordsworth enjoyed questioning intelligent children on serious subjects, usually of an ethical or moral nature. Childhood intuition was to be an important part of his theory of human life, as you will see in this and the following poem. In his famous *Ode* (*'There was a time'*) he was to describe the Child as *Mighty Prophet! Seer Blest!* (line 114). Coleridge disagreed severely with this view of childhood. You may find it useful to consider his objection.

> What does all this mean? In what sense is a child of that age a *philosopher*? In what sense is he declared to be for *ever haunted* by the Supreme Being? Or so inspired as to deserve the splendid titles of a mighty prophet, a blessed seer? By reflection! By knowledge! By conscious intuition! Children at this age give us no information of themselves: and at what time were we dipped in the Lethe which has produced such utter oblivion of a state so godlike?...In what sense can the magnificent attributes, above quoted, be appropriated to a *child*, which would not make them equally suitable to a *bee*, or a *dog*, or a *field of corn*, or even to a ship, or to the wind and waves that propel it? The omnipresent Spirit works equally in *them* as in the child; and the child is equally unconscious of it as they.

> (*BL*, Ch. XXII, pp. 222–3)

Do you agree with Coleridge's objection to Wordsworth's exaltation of childhood innocence? Wordsworth is not the only poet to idealize childhood. The Metaphysical Poets of the seventeenth century spoke of childhood as a time of divine vision, but Wordsworth is in dangerous waters when he attempts to endow childhood with a sense of conscious wisdom or reflection. What he is appreciating is a freshness of *sight*; wonder unclouded by worldly cynicism. His old men and women sometimes return to this experience of the world, but after passing through suffering to reach a passive acceptance of the world as it is, not as they would like it to be.

 10 **Kilve** a village on the Bristol Channel.
13–14 This may allude, in contrast, to those painful days on returning from France when Wordsworth could not bear to think about the difficulties of public and private morality.
 24 **Liswyn Farm** on the Wye near Hay-on-Wye. Thelwall farmed at Llyswen.

The poet's attempt to force Edward to say why he prefers Kilve to Liswyn results in a lie (because the latter has a weathercock) invented merely to placate the questioner. Wordsworth seems chastened by the reply, but what deep truth is revealed is hard to detect.

We Are Seven

This poem was composed in the spring of 1798 while Wordsworth was walking in the grove at Alfoxden, five years after meeting a little girl in the grounds of Goodrich Castle during his tour of the Wye Valley. It deals with *the perplexity and obscurity which in childhood attend our notion of death, or rather our utter inability to admit that notion* (Wordsworth's Preface of 1800; see Appendices, p. 231). Wordsworth described his own childhood in such terms. Later he was to use this experience as grounds for a belief in immortality. There is some contradiction between his Pantheistic belief in nature and a belief in pre-existence. His interest in the child's stubborn insistence that the family remains undivided may be prompted by his admiration of the girl's absolute belief in her own convictions (Wordsworth was equally dogmatic) and his idealization of the family unit. His love for his sister, his grief over the death at sea of his brother and the early death of his daughter Dora powerfully influenced his life, strengthening his convictions on the importance of the family.

The form of 8 syllable/6 syllable lines with alternate rhymes is a popular folk structure. Wordsworth's obsession with numbers – *two at Conway dwell, Two of us in the churchyard lie, Twelve steps or more* – may seem tedious, and the poem has been much criticized for its sentimentality. The notion that two siblings lie fully conscious in the grave, a place that he would describe later as *a place of thought where we in waiting lie* (see the *Ode on the Intimations of Immortality*) is certainly morbid. Coleridge found it horrifying.

Verse 1   This suggests that the child is almost entirely concerned with its physical body.
9–10   She was obliged to wear cast-offs from other siblings.

Because of its sentimentality, this poem damaged Wordsworth's reputation. In fact, both Wordsworth and Coleridge were later satirized for their obvious fondness for children. You might like to take some time here to consider the difference between sentiment and sentimentality.

Lines Written in Early Spring

This famous poem, with its striking first line, was composed in a grove beside the brook at Alfoxden. Imagine an enclosed scene of diffused light; an interplay of wind and falling water. Art and nature seem entwined in picturesque beauty. In a note he dictated to Isabella Fenwick, Wordsworth records a particular ash tree that captures something of the spirit of this scene (perhaps the same ash tree recorded in Coleridge's *This Lime Tree Bower my Prison*). It shows Wordsworth's wonderful eye for detail.

> ...a fallen ash from which rose perpendicularly boughs in search of the light intercepted by the deep shade above. The boughs bore leaves of green that for want of sunshine had faded into almost lily-white; and, from the underside of this natural sylvan bridge depended long and beautiful tresses of ivy which waved gently in the breeze that might poetically speaking be called the breath of the waterfall.

The opening line of the poem perfectly captures this sense of things interfused; a harmony, as in music, of the elements of air, light, water, sound and scent. A simple eight-foot line with alternate rhyme seems perfectly tuned to the voice. Wordsworth does not try to teach us a lesson. The mood is relaxed, reflective and human. It is a delicately crafted, profound poem reflecting one man's intimate relationship with nature. Here we have an example of Wordsworth's Pantheism at its purest. God *is* nature and man only a part of that vast organism.

Verse 1 Why do pleasant thoughts evoke sad ones?

Verse 2 A number of ideas are interwoven here. Shocked that his country had failed to support the revolution in France, Wordsworth re-examined his radical views after witnessing the upheaval and brutality which followed what he had conceived as a struggle for freedom. The thought goes deeper than mere political events, conveying uncertainty as to man's place in the scheme of nature, his fall from grace and moral goodness.

Verse 3 Primrose and periwinkle are wild flowers; Wordsworth disliked cultivated ones.

Verse 5 Each tiny twig seems an active player in the organism, spreading its fan to catch the air. (Cf. Coleridge's *airy harps* in *The Nightingale*, line 82.)

   22 **my creed** Are we able at this stage to say exactly what Wordsworth's creed is?

The Thorn

Wordsworth's longest poem in the collection is a dramatic monologue. Some characters have resemblance to known persons. Basil Montagu's mother was called Martha Ray and she was murdered by a spurned lover. There are hints also of the life of Mary Wollstonecraft, author of *The Vindications of the Rights of Women* (1792), who twice attempted suicide because of the unfaithfulness of her lover.

The poem was written quickly on 19 March 1798 and, according to Wordsworth, arose, *out of my observing on the edge of Quantock Hill on a sunny day, a thorn which I have often passed in calm and bright weather*. The weather was stormy and the lonely image of this stunted tree affected him deeply. The narrator is a loquacious sea-captain. Coleridge later observed that it is difficult to imitate a garrulous style without repeating the effects. Stories of deserted women are legion in literature, and madness induced by rejection was to be a favourite theme of later writers. Though Wordsworth was no feminist, his work had the effect of drawing attention to the peculiar difficulties of impoverished women.

4–5   In what ways are the thorn and the child connected?

9–11   The thorn is a symbol of endurance.

27, 29, 33   **five yards...three yards...three feet long, and two feet wide**. As in guidebooks of the day, Wordsworth wishes to direct us to the exact spot. Line 33 has been much criticized and debated.

40–41   Though of humble stock, Martha has created a memorial garden of living lacework reminiscent of the fine needlework of medieval ladies.

Verse 5   This somewhat morbid preoccupation with death and children was a feature of the poetry of the Graveyard School of the eighteenth century, of which Gray's *Elegy* is the most prominent example. (See *Lines Written near Richmond, upon the Thames, at Evening*.) It was to become a prominent feature in literature of the nineteenth century. Consider some of the reasons why this morbidity should take such a strong hold of the Romantic imagination.

65   The refrain '*Oh misery! Oh misery!*' captures Martha's extreme bereavement. Words depicting various shades of sadness – *doleful, dreary, woe, melancholy, forlorn* – are frequent.

Verse 7   The simple beauty of this passage shows the perfect use of the ballad form. Most of the words are monosyllabic – *star, wind, air, hill, skies*. The expression can hardly be considered to be the *real language of men* for the thought is complex. Martha becomes an integral part of the universe. Wordsworth introduced this idea of the sublime into the Romantic consciousness.

90   **no one knows**   The uncertainty as to whether or not Martha kills her child is important. (For a subtle reading of the poem see John F. Danby, *The Simple Wordsworth*, Routledge and Kegan Paul, 1960, pp. 57–72.)

Verses 11–12   reveal the cause of Martha's lunacy: her desertion by Stephen Hill.

Verse 16   There are curious omissions in this story. For example, is the churchyard near the mountain peak? Does Martha speak with ghosts?

188–191   Once again the wind has mystical connections. Martha is associated with gales, as if her madness at such times is at its height. Even the pond is said to shake with little breezes.

214–216   That Martha may have hanged her child on the thorn or drowned it gives added horror. There are said to be drops of the infant's blood on the moss; the grass is said to shiver; men come with spades to dig for the child's bones but are repelled by fearful signs. These things hint at the supernatural but are also the stuff of folk tales. The Moors Murders in the 1960s, which caused public controversy for decades, were, in a sense, surrounded by similar superstitions; clearly such sentiments are deeply enshrined in the public imagination.

Consider why the poem is called *The Thorn* and not *Martha Ray*. Why do the mosses try to pull the thorn down? What motivates Martha – revenge, innocence, guilt, or some other power? Is the poem a success poetically or just a stirring tale? Coleridge criticized it for not fulfilling Wordsworth's own criteria of low and rustic life, insisting that such tragedies are universal, but Wordsworth is arguing that country life brings people closer to nature, exposing them to the extremes of weather and more lonely suffering. Unfortunately, his condemnation of the city and his idealization of country life led him to ignore some of the degrading effects of life without books or conversation, or the sophistications of an urban environment.

The Last of the Flock

This poem is based on the case of a Holford farmer, denied poor relief and obliged to sell off his flock in order to feed his large family. It challenges Godwin's theory that the possession of private property is a source of evil. Wordsworth believed poor relief should not be punitive. The Poor Law Amendment Act of 1834 would abolish outdoor relief altogether so that no able-bodied person could claim relief without going to the workhouse, an institution that soon acquired fearful associations because it separated families into male and female. Produced in 1798, at the same time as *The Complaint of a Forsaken Indian Woman*, this poem records Wordsworth's repulsion at those laws which break family bonds. Superficially the shepherd's action is unmanly, but he is carrying a lamb – which has clear Christian connotations with the Good Shepherd.

11 **he saw me and he turned aside** expresses the man's simple dignity.

13–14 This small detail is a beautifully observed example (copied by Chekhov in his short story *The Student*) of how sometimes literalness can create an exquisite touch of reality. It is worth reflecting on the numerous references to tears in *Lyrical*

Ballads: in *Simon Lee*, *tears into his eyes were brought* (line 97); in *The Female Vagrant* the last lines record her weeping; in *Lines Left upon a Seat in a Yew-tree* the man's eyes *streamed with tears* (line 42); in *The Idiot Boy* Betty weeps *Such tears she never shed before* (line 308); the convict in the poem of the same name weeps (line 42); and in *The Nightingale* we are given a description of a child's tears glittering in the moonlight. Weeping is caused by sorrow and joy, a combination explored in *The Idiot Boy*.

Verses 3–4   describe the shepherd's fortunes in youth. From a single ewe his flock increases to fifty. His family also multiplies. They are a single entity upon which nature smiles. The simple language of the shepherd here is the true naturalness for which Wordsworth continually strives. We are not told why the shepherd's fortunes fail but it would seem that his sheep feed on the mountain pastures, technically common land, and such property can be reclaimed. He is refused relief and even made to feel guilty: *'how can we give to you,'/They cried, 'what to the poor is due?'* (lines 49–50).

63–64   Astonishingly daring but beautiful lines. The agonizing decline in the flock to one inevitable end increases the shepherd's sense of helplessness. References to blood in Wordsworth are always interesting – another aspect of the family bond. Blood implies *heart* – a powerful symbol physically and emotionally. In *Tintern Abbey* Wordsworth argues that feelings such as pity, joy and beauty can actually change the physical body.

Verses 8–9   Now nature seems to curse him.

91–100   The exact figures graphically describe how the flock dwindles. The calculation here seems perfectly judged, in contrast with those in *The Thorn* and *We Are Seven*. The simple ending is poignant. We are left not knowing what will happen to the shepherd though we guess it will be that destitution which the law demands before any award of charity can be granted.

The Last of the Flock is a moving and entirely human poem. The tone in this poem seems perfectly judged, the rhythms of natural speech beautifully articulated, while the moral is implied rather than proclaimed. Paradoxically, such *naturalness* is very difficult to achieve. Delicate poetic effects are not produced without great labour. Wordsworth is trying to define aspects of human life which are subtle and obscure. Though he is not always successful, he is working in a new medium for poetry and his originality in this field is unquestioned.

The Dungeon

Man was born free, yet everywhere he is in chains. These words from Rousseau's *Social Contract* (1763) embody the spirit of the Romantic Movement on the theme of man's inhumanity, among them this further extract from Coleridge's *Osorio* and Wordsworth's *The Convict*. Both believed that the unwilling confinement of any sentient being is evil. The cruelty implied here includes all penal punishment. The fall of the Bastille soon acquired symbolic importance as an attack on political tyranny. Though part of a play, this extract is meaningful as a separate entity and is an expression of Coleridge's moral outrage at man's pitiless cruelty.

    1 an exclamation of horror at what *man has made of man* (see *Lines Written in Early Spring*, line 8).

  4–5 **and what if guilty?/Is this the only cure? Merciful God!** You will recognize at once Coleridge's rhetorical style with its questions and exclamations.

 6–11 **each pore and natural outlet shrivell'd up** (see Wordsworth's *Our minds shall drink at every pore*, from *Lines, Written a Small Distance from my House*, line 27). The prisoner's natural instincts are tortured by pain and isolation and the result is madness. Many of the images in the poem are about disease – *stagnates, corrupts, poison, plague, distempered*.

  11 **pamper'd mountebanks** rich lawyers.

20–30 The last section suggests that nature can minister to a wild and angry heart. Through love and beauty and by hearing what Wordsworth calls later *the still, sad music of humanity*, vice and misery are healed. Through the expression of emotion, a return to repentance and final forgiveness is achieved.

The Mad Mother

The subject was reported to me by a lady of Bristol who had seen the poor creature. So wrote Wordsworth in the notes he dictated to Isabella Fenwick. The combination of motherhood and madness is irresistible to his imagination and in this poem he creates something symbolic of a Madonna and Child, though set in the daring context of destitution combined with mental illness – as commonplace in his day as it continues to be in ours.

The ten-line stanza, with its three pairs of rhyming couplets enclosing two pairs of alternate rhymes, and the final two lines of each stanza having three rhymes, is ingenious, giving a balanced song-like structure which is the essence of the ballad form. There are two kinds of ballads in Wordsworth's canon: those where, as Hazlitt observes in *The Spirit of the Age* (1825), he uses an incident or character primarily as a peg on which to hang a moral – *Simon Lee*, *Goody Blake and Harry Gill* and *We Are Seven* – and those distinguished by Keats where *he thinks into the human heart* – *The Last of the Flock, Old Man Travelling, The Vagrant Woman* and *The Mad Mother* – poems in which Wordsworth has created real human figures whose deep, yet simple, affections are closely and movingly observed.

1–4 **Her eyes are wild, her head is bare**   is a vivid visual image of the woman. She looks foreign – possibly Spanish or Indian (see *I'll build an Indian bower*, line 55) – though she speaks English.

21–23 These lines describe her hallucinations and have a strange manic quality in keeping with her deranged state of mind.

28 **My little boy of flesh and blood**   represents the interaction of mind and body. In line 32 we are told that the suckling babe affects the woman's mental state.

39–40 These lines make the same connection between derangement and the wind as in *The Thorn*. They were much commended by Coleridge as

...so expressive of that deranged state, in which from the increased sensibility the sufferer's attention is abruptly drawn off by every trifle, and in the same instant plucked back again by the one despotic thought, bringing home with it, by the blending, fusing power of Imagination and Passion, the alien object to which it had been so abruptly diverted, no longer an alien but an ally and an intimate.

(*BL*, Ch. XXII, p. 231)

Verse 5 Consider the repeated reference to the four elements – earth, air, fire and water. The woman's sensibilities seem acutely sensitive to their influences.

50 As with Betty Foy and her idiot boy, there is an intimate bond between mother and child. The mother is also a child because she has little understanding of the appalling sadness of her situation.

61 As with Martha Ray, the woman has been abandoned by the father of her child, but is still seeking him among the woods to disprove the stigma of illegitimacy.

89 **If thou art mad, my pretty lad**   is a cruel reminder of hereditary madness.

99–100 The poem closes on a note of pastoral idyll. In her fantasy world there is no tragic ending, but the reader knows only too well *the poisons of the shade*.

The Idiot Boy

In this extended narrative Wordsworth attempts an even more difficult exploration of mental disturbance. The subject of the poem suffers from idiocy, a condition which, in the light of Betty Foy's age, we might now describe as Down's Syndrome. The theme has marvellous artistic power and was to inspire many later writers, particularly the Russian novelist Fyodor Dostoevsky (1821–1881), whose work *The Idiot* is a study of a Christ-like being, subject to epileptic fits, who has visions of a greater reality. The child in Wordsworth's poem also possesses unusual powers of apprehension. Lacking all sense of time, Johnny is unable to order events in sequence. He lives in fragments. In his innocence he has never learned to judge or reject; therefore he shines out above the other characters who embody a stream of shifting and often ill-judged impressions. Wordsworth stakes everything on a simple, straightforward narrative – short declarative statements with frequent time shifts. The psychological states of Betty and Susan are closely observed. In focusing on the poem's faults, Coleridge failed to appreciate the huge psychological and artistic potential in this exploration of a new and untried level of poetic experience.

The poem was written in March 1798. In a note he dictated to Isabella Fenwick, Wordsworth added *I never wrote anything with so much glee*, perhaps because it describes again the extremes of emotion. He intended Johnny's final words – *The cocks did crow, and the sun did shine so cold* – to be the central idea of the poem, but the line is enigmatic. Cocks are said to crow at sunrise, and there is a connection with this and the denial of Christ by Peter. The obvious Christian moral of the good neighbour is also implied, but there are a number of recurring images – moonlight, owls, water, references to folk tales – which give the poem a wider mythological range. The poem is uneven in quality. Parts are deliberately comic; others satirical, even visionary; and there is an attempt at the mock-heroic. There are echoes of Robert

Notes

Burns's *Tam o Shanter* (1791), the story of a drunken Scotsman
pursued home by the devil and saved by his horse. Look
carefully at Wordsworth's use of metre. Does it aid or hinder
him in creating an imitation of the real language of men? What
happens to such ordinary language when it is made to conform
to a regular metre?

Wordsworth would always stand by this poem which had
given him so much pleasure to write and insisted on its inclusion
in later editions. It is essential to see the poem as a critical
challenge, an experiment in a new and difficult medium.

14 **fiddle-faddle** a colloquial word for muddle. There are many
other such words in the poem: *hurly-burly, to-whoo, to-whoo!,
rap, rap, rap!, halloo! halloo!* What effect do these homespun
words have?

16 It is common for mothers to show particular love for the
weakest child in the family, especially an only child born to
older parents. In line 289 we learn that Betty is *almost three-
score* years old.

19 **His lips with joy they burr at you** describes a sound of
pleasure.

Verse 5 Betty's decision to send Johnny for the doctor is foolish but
unselfish. She has strong maternal pride in Johnny. If owls
are wise, there is something of the cock's crowing in her
anticipation of his *glory*.

43 Only the pony shows the virtues of patience and stability. He
literally carries the action.

Verse 12 **boot...whip...spur...the holly bough** instruments of
chastisement, a further interesting comparison of the idea of
Christ-like patience in the pony.

61 Holly is a plant said to give protection against evil spirits.

169–189 '**A little, idle sauntering thing!**' Betty's words show her
volatile change of view. The poem is a study in female
emotion. Her counting the hours of the clock and her
premature fears increase the tension.

225 This image suggests visual instability, drunkenness and
lunacy.

Verse 35–37 The countryside described is typical of the Quantocks.

164

Betty's imagination runs riot on natural and supernatural dangers.

247 **distemper** a feverish condition brought on here by a disturbance of mind. In her distraction Betty's actions seem comic.

Verses 41–45 Betty's rapping at the door, the doctor's appearance at the window, his annoyance and Betty's *Woe is me!* have all the ingredients of eighteenth-century pictorial comedy.

Verses 46–58 contain the extreme stages of Betty's hysteria – from pride to suicide.

307–308 Almost every poem of Wordsworth's in *Lyrical Ballads* includes weeping.

311 **And we will ne'er o'erload thee more**. This promise to the pony is beautifully observed because in line 251 Betty had rained curses on his head.

330–331 Johnny's fancies are all associated with the moon and stars.

408 Betty's verdict implies the relativity of all action. He had failed completely but to her his efforts are heroic.

425–426 Susan forgets her ailments, *as if by magic cured* (line 436), in her anxiety for the child's safety.

Verse 78 Why should the owls have played an important role?

460–461 Johnny muddles the owl's cry with that of the cock, but what other significance is implied? The child Edward in *Anecdote for Fathers* also refers to the cock.

Johnny's cryptic utterance may represent time recovered but neither focused nor understood. His refusal to tell his story leaves the reader's imagination in possession of a number of possibilities. Was he cared for by natural spirits (the moon and stars, the pony), by supernatural ones (fairies or goblins), or by pure chance? Because he is maladjusted, Johnny, like the Mad Mother, lives mostly in his dreams and fancies and is protected from disaster by being outside the normal experiences of logical cause and effect. Whatever the interpretation, Wordsworth has created an intriguing story which, in spite of its technical flaws, was to capture the imagination of later writers.

Lines Written near Richmond, upon the Thames, at Evening

This poem probably dates from 1789 when Wordsworth was at Cambridge, and the river described originally was the Cam. Such an early, pensive poem is useful in showing how *Lyrical Ballads* is not an abrupt departure from the neo-classical tradition of the eighteenth century. Rather, it shows how Wordsworth's teacher, the Revd William Taylor, had conveyed a love of the Graveyard School of poets (including Thomas Gray, Thomas Chatterton, Edward Young and William Collins) whose sweet, emotional styles were employed in musings on the themes of melancholy and death. The poem is central to Wordsworth's later theory of emotion recollected in tranquillity. Two favourite themes, rivers and evening, are brought together. Make a list of all those poems in *Lyrical Ballads* that describe these two themes.

1–8   Wordsworth muses on the water at sunset as seen from a boat sailing into the *crimson west*. He is aware that the *backward stream*, which seconds before had seemed so fair and might be so still to *some other loiterer beguiling*, now appears dark and threatening. The themes of time, loss and illusion so beloved of Collins are considered. There is a Romantic pose in the thought that, like Thomas Chatterton who committed suicide at the age of eighteen, Wordsworth too might *die in sorrow*. This theme was to preoccupy nineteenth-century poets until, in its final decades, suicide became an almost aesthetic necessity!

17   **Glide gently, thus for ever glide**   is an imitation of the mellifluous assonance we hear in Collins. With its soft, feminine rhymes, the whole verse is very different from the style of most of the poems in *Lyrical Ballads*. Why might Wordsworth, while retaining so much of the sentiment of the Graveyard School, later try to free himself from its style?

27   Why should a fast-flowing river be like a poet's heart? Wordsworth recalls the death of James Thomson (1700–1748), buried at Richmond.

29–36   These lines refer to Collins's sad and penniless later years.
The reference to *tears, which Love and Pity shed* (Collins's *Ode on the Death of Mr Thomson*, stanza 6; note the capital letters used in the two abstract nouns) is central to Wordsworth's philosophy of the human heart.

37–40   A sense of grave stillness, disturbed only by the dripping of oars, closes the poem. That *holy time* of twilight – a phrase used by Coleridge – descends.

The poem, suggestive of a young poet learning his craft, is technically impressive. The iambic metre is made more lyrical by the use of enjambement, while the lovely feminine rhymes[2] – *smiling/beguiling, sorrow/to-morrow, bestowing/flowing, suspended/attended* – characterize time and the river in their everflowing onward movement.

Expostulation and Reply

Composed in the spring of 1798, this poem may be compared with *Lines Left upon a Seat in A Yew-tree* in that it deals with the subject of nature as a source of comfort and visionary power. The setting is the Lake District. Wordsworth describes himself as a dreamer content to spend half a day in solitary contemplation. The character Matthew, mentioned in line 13, is Hazlitt, who found Wordsworth's dismissal of metaphysical speculation and science annoying, hence the question: *Where are your books? That light bequeath'd / To beings else forlorn and blind!* (lines 5–6).

Expostulation   means hypothesis or argument
Verse 5   Wordsworth is concerned with the senses and the emotions rather than the intellect. The sense that appears most strongly

---

[2] A technical term used for rhymes of usually two or three syllables in which only the first syllable is stressed.

in his work is sight – looking, gazing, weeping, blindness, and all things connected with the eyes. We are constantly given *pictures* – people and objects in a landscape. Though no one would deny that Wordsworth was a man of profound feeling, he was no philosopher and here he distinguishes between mind and sense in a simplistic Cartesian manner, arguing that the senses are instinctive and intuitive and therefore superior to the intellectual arguments of *dead men* (line 8). The *wise passiveness* in line 24 echoes the argument in *Lines, written at a Small Distance from my House*, where he asserts that *fifty years of reason* (line 26) are inferior to one moment of communion with nature. It is questionable whether the ballad form with its unsubtle rhyme scheme is a suitable medium for philosophical analysis. That Coleridge encouraged Wordsworth to consider himself as a philosopher-poet is a sad consequence of their friendship.

The Tables Turned

This is Wordsworth's more considered development of the idea in the previous poem and contains his view that nature is the greatest teacher (line 26).

21–24   **vernal**   spring. Wordsworth adds morality to the teachings of nature. This is a contentious argument for it is questionable that nature has any moral foundation whatsoever; rather, it is a vast and impersonal system external to the social world of human action and responsibility.

Verse 7   Wordsworth is on more convincing ground here. Like the German Romantic poet, scientist and philosopher Johann Wolfgang von Goethe (1770–1834), whose work is a much more sophisticated attack on the mechanical probing of the material sciences into the creative forces at work in nature, Wordsworth argues that nature's *beauteous forms* are illusive, soul-like bodies which are destroyed in the very act of analysis. Coleridge was completely in agreement with this

view, believing the speculative mind in isolation to be totally
arid. To argue that both science and art are *barren leaves* (line
30) is extreme. Nevertheless, there is a huge and complex idea
of organic form at the heart of these four lines which has
great resonance in both philosophy and aesthetics. That both
poets communed with each other – Coleridge providing
Wordsworth with a coherent intellectual system and
Wordsworth appearing to Coleridge as an example of the
visionary poet – is one of the most fascinating aspects of
Lyrical Ballads. Wordsworth held fast to his creed, seeming
unable or unwilling to enter into Coleridge's more abstract
world.

Old Man Travelling

This is a reflective and profound poem on old age, written in
1797. In *Fenwick Notes* Wordsworth writes: *If I recollect aright,
these verses were an overflowing from 'The Old Cumberland Beggar'*
(p. 57). He chooses to write in blank verse avoiding rhymes that
seem awkward in poems such as *Simon Lee*. Whereas Simon Lee
is senile, this old man, *subdued to settled quiet*, has achieved
dignity and heroism. The title is important. The man is *travelling*,
yet has acquired stillness in the face of adversity – a figure in a
landscape, still and still moving. Wordsworth's solitaries are at
the extremes of life – early childhood, lunacy, blindness, idiocy
or destitution. Under such pressures, people become strangely
universal yet uniquely themselves. A man out in all weathers, he
just keeps going, reminding us of other great solitaries such as
Oedipus and Lear.

   1–2 The symbol of the hedgerow birds has a biblical resonance
         suggesting innocence, humility and harmony with nature.
         Here the old man's silent passing does not disturb their
         feeding. He seems less important than they.
   6–7 **A man who does not move with pain, but moves/ With**

thought For Wordsworth, reflection always takes place in solitude. Unlike Coleridge, who dreaded solitude, Wordsworth actively enjoyed loneliness, undertaking long and exhausting walks in the Lake District even in extreme old age. Hazlitt wrote of him: *It is as if there were nothing but himself and the universe. He lives in the busy solitude of his own heart: in the deep silence of thought* (*Selected Writings*, ed. R. Blythe, Penguin, 1970, p. 59). The old man has passed through pain into peace. Now he just *is*, the embodiment of patient humanity achieving that *central peace, subsisting at the heart/Of endless agitation* (Wordsworth, *The Excursion*, Book IV, lines 1146–7).

13–14 A comparison with youth dramatizes the old man's timeless dignity. Unaware of the purgatorial experience he has endured, the old man has a truly tragic stature.

15–20 The final lines deal with the man's destination. Touching as these lines are, and hinting at the son's patriotic duty, the detail seems unnecessary and in later editions Wordsworth abandoned these lines.

In studying the poem you will see that there is a preponderance of monosyllabic nouns – *birds, pack, face, step, gait, look, pain, thought, limb* – and a corresponding lack of adjectives. Percy Bysshe Shelley spoke of Wordsworth awakening *a sort of thought in sense*. The comment is apt. Where he is didactic or consciously philosophizing, Wordsworth becomes pompous. This poem shows his strength where, through the recollection of deep feeling, objects and people acquire a mystical quality which is the product of meditation. Coleridge does not do him full justice when he describes Wordsworth's tendency to be a *spectator ab extra* (*Table Talk*, 31 July 1832), a possible development of his 'tourist's eye'. He was not interested in God, theology or philosophy, but in man, nature and morality. See the section on 'The still, sad music of humanity' in Interpretations, pages 186–93.

The Complaint of a Forsaken Indian Woman

The long sub-title is taken from Samuel Hearne's *A Journey from Prince of Wales Fort in Hudson's Bay to the Northern Ocean* (1795; ed. J.B. Tyrrell, The Chaplain Society, 1911). This story of the approaching death through consumption of the wife of an Indian who has been abandoned with provisions – not from cruelty but from necessity, the tribe having to move on because of the cold weather – made a deep impact on Wordsworth. Women figure prominently in his character studies and at least four suffer from some kind of mental derangement. This woman is left in complete solitude and her helplessness is appalling. Her child has been taken from her, her fire dies, her water freezes and wolves have stolen her food. No human soul is left to share her last agonies of mind and body. It is difficult to conceive of a more extreme form of suffering. Wordsworth, as all Romantic poets, was fascinated by death, and here confronts the very moment which he feels to be a state almost unimaginable. In looking back at his childhood, Wordsworth acknowledged:

> Nothing was more difficult for me in childhood than to admit the notion of death as a state applicable to my own being... I used to brood over the stories of Enoch and Elijah, and almost persuade myself that, whatever might become of others, I should be translated, in something of the same way to heaven...

> I was often unable to think of external things as having external existence, and I communed with all that I saw as something not apart from, but inherent in, my own immaterial nature. Many times while going to school have I grasped at a wall or tree to recall myself from this abyss of idealism to reality.

> (*Fenwick Notes*, p. 61)

Unlike the old man in the previous poem who continues travelling, the woman here has no more strength. Her thoughts fluctuate between hope and despair, hallucination and sanity. She blames herself for her lack of strength; then she blames others for her desertion. The phrase *too soon*, used three times, echoes her final regrets on earth.

Verse 4 dwells on the parting with her child. This strong and intimate maternal bond is deliberately severed.

There are some fine lines, such as *The stars they were among my dreams* (line 4), but overall the poem seems rather lifeless and repetitive. The idea is striking and original, but the emotion expressed is perhaps a little too extreme.

The Convict

Many of the poems in *Lyrical Ballads* involve punishment – the punishment of the poor by the rich, disease, age, madness or social discrimination, or the self-punishment of guilt. The literature of prisons and convicts in the nineteenth century is a major study in itself. In this poem Wordsworth considers the penal system, a topic of current debate arising from Godwin, who had argued in *Political Justice* that life-imprisonment or deportation to the colonies were preferable to capital punishment. Compare these sentiments with Coleridge's in *The Dungeon*. Written in 1793, this poem shows Wordsworth's republicanism.

The form is striking – alternately rhyming lines of 11/8–9 feet and a song-like rhythm. It is difficult to achieve naturalness in such a strong ballad metre, yet Wordsworth produces a moving lament on the inhumanity of prison conditions and a picture of a man at his wit's end. Such cruelty is society's thirst for revenge, not reform.

Verse 1   A glorious sunset makes more painful the experience of the
           second verse when he must face a dreaded visit to the
           convict.

rses 6–10 contain stark images of a bodily nature – hair, head,
           shoulders, visage, bones, blood, limbs, eyes, all wracked.
           Equally tormented are heart, soul, mind, imagination and
           conscience – agonies seen in the *Ancyent Marinere*. Guilt and
           shame have corroded every human aspect of the convict's
           existence; an unrelenting torment, which sickens the poet.

ses 12–13 are an appeal for compassion. Wordsworth comes to the
           scene as *a brother thy sorrows to share* (line 48). Lines 51–52
           deliver the final statement: '*My care, if the arm of the mighty
           were mine,/Would plant thee where yet thou might'st blossom
           again*'; that is, transportation to the colonies. The images of
           planting and blossoming are characteristic of Wordsworth
           taking his images from nature wherever possible.

The poem immediately precedes his masterpiece *Lines Written a
Few Miles above Tintern Abbey* where we are shown not, as here, a
man crushed by society, excluded even from nature's benign and
healing powers, but the poet himself enjoying warm human
companionship at the heart of nature's powers of *tranquil
restoration*.

Lines Written a Few Miles above
Tintern Abbey

Lyrical Ballads ends with one of Wordsworth's most
accomplished odes, described in a later version of the Preface as
written *with a hope that in the transitions, and the impassioned music
of the versification would be found the principal requisites of that
species of composition*. Consider the ode as a summation of
Wordsworth's work in the collection. First read the poem,
bearing in mind some of the themes that you have studied:

- the role of time in the maturing of our thoughts and feelings
- the influence of nature as a teacher, source of joy, consolation and visionary power
- those *little, nameless, unremembered acts/Of kindness and of love* (lines 35–36)
- Wordsworth's thoughts on the family.

This poem comes as close to religious feeling as anything in Wordsworth's work. It is impossible to interpret the poem as religious in any orthodox way unless one were to consider something of the nature of Buddhist meditation. Partly through Wordsworth's use of blank verse, the poem combines Classic calm with Romantic excitement. The figure in a landscape is the poet and the landscape is also an inner one – recovering pleasure or *emotion recollected in tranquillity*.

1 **Five years have passed** 1793–1798. These years were ones of fundamental change in Wordsworth's political views.

3 The use of the word *rolling* conveys a timeless process connecting different forms of nature.

9–11 **when I again repose/Here, under this dark sycamore, and view/These plots of cottage-ground** This view, looking out onto a sunlit scene, has the painter's perspective of the period. The artistic tourist would sometimes carry a Claude Lorrain glass[3], or mirror, to compose a picturesque scene.

13–18 The copses and hedgerows – *sportive wood run wild* – have a dynamic quality of movement. The word *green* occurs three times in five lines.

18–19 **wreathes of smoke/Sent up, in silence, from among the trees** are probably from the fires of charcoal burners.

25 **blind man's eye** We have seen how Wordsworth frequently refers to the sense of sight. He seems a spectator in his great *Ode on the Intimations of Immortality* (1807), where he employs a symbol of wisdom *as an eye/That hath kept watch oe'r man's*

---

[3] Claude Lorrain (1600–1682), a French landscape painter who used a lens to frame his compositions.

mortality. This has suggestions of oriental mysticism and much of the second paragraph conveys a trance-like state of mind close to that experienced in Buddhist meditation.

29–30   We have seen how the word *blood* has rich associations. In lines 45–50 Wordsworth extends the thought. This section is justly famous as the heart of Wordsworth's philosophy. He suggests that mind can actually *change* the physical body.

One can see why, as a philosopher, Coleridge found Wordsworth's use of words such as *blood, power, heart, body, soul* and *life* vague, but Wordsworth is attempting to convey a kind of spiritual transcendentalism; what the Indian mystic calls *sartori.* In lines 38–42 he refers to something in the soul more sublime than intellect, inspired by nature, increasing our sense of wonder at the majesty of the universe and transporting us out of the body. In one of his letters, Keats refers to this lifting of *the burthen of the mystery* as a critical point in human life. His examination of this section of Wordsworth's ode is striking and illuminating:

I compare human life to a large Mansion of many apartments, two of which I can only describe, the doors of the rest being as yet shut upon me. The first we step into we call the Infant, or Thoughtless Chamber, in which we remain as long as we do not think. We remain there a long while, and not withstanding the doors of the second Chamber remain wide open, showing a bright appearance, we care not to hasten to it; but are at length imperceptibly impelled by the awakening of the thinking principle within us – we no sooner get into the second Chamber, which I shall call the Chamber of Maiden Thought, than we become intoxicated with the light and the atmosphere, we see nothing but pleasant wonders, and think of delaying there for ever in delight. However, among the effects this breathing is father of is that tremendous one of sharpening one's vision into the heart and nature of Man – of convincing one's nerves that the world is full of Misery and Heartbreak, Pain, Sickness and oppression – whereby this Chamber of Maiden Thought becomes gradually darkened, and at the same time, on all sides of it, many doors are set open – but all dark – all leading to dark passages.

> We see not the balance of good and evil; we are in a mist, we are
> now in that state we feel the *Burden of the Mystery*. To this point
> was Wordsworth come, as far as I can conceive, when he wrote
> Tintern Abbey, and it seems to me that his genius is explorative
> of those dark Passages.

(Keats, 'Letter to Reynolds', 3 May 1818, in Keats: Poetry and Prose,
ed. H. Ellershaw, Clarendon Press, 1956, p. 173)

Keats sees the *burthen of the mystery* as a moment when the ego
seems deserted by nature, lonely and afraid, almost as a severing
of a kind of umbilical cord between mother and child. The *fever
of the world* threatens to break the heart; we are *in a mist* (the echo
of Coleridge is obvious) but *another nature* appears, one that is
part of the moral nature of man and is underpinned by
unremembered acts/Of kindness and of love (lines 35–36). This
conveys *a serene and blessed mood* (line 42), one that only appears
when the man of feeling has also thought long and deeply. It
seems to contradict what Wordsworth tells us about childhood.
It is a paradox which he never succeeded in resolving.

Wordsworth continues to examine how time has changed the
initial impression of the scene. In revisiting the Wye Valley with
Dorothy he has recovered not only past pleasures, but food for
future years through her pleasure.

67–86 His first relationship with nature was physical. The period
has passed. *And all its aching joys are now no more.*

92 **The still, sad, music of humanity**   This idea is explored in
Interpretations, pages 186–93. Time takes away the
unencumbered joys of childhood. This is more than loss of
innocence. Wordsworth believes that not only does man
change in the course of his earthly existence but *the whole
earth* has changed. He and Coleridge believed that mankind
was losing a power of vision to see into the heart of reality.
A divine grace had vanished from the earth. Nature might be
man's nurse, guardian and joy, but it is in essence
impenetrable. What separates Coleridge and Wordsworth is
that, as a Christian, Coleridge believes that body, soul and

spirit are separate entities, the highest being the spirit, whereas for Wordsworth, these three are one. We call Wordsworth's philosophy *Monism* (oneness). For Coleridge, the *language of the sense* and *all the mighty world of eye and ear* are not enough. Man is given reason, and from this stems the whole world of thought, morality and science.

The final paragraph of the poem moves from Wordsworth to Dorothy, in whose pleasure he detects his own former bliss – *what I was once* (line 121). It conveys his profound love for her.

120 **thy wild eyes**   You will recall the opening lines of *The Mad Mother*. How this applies to Dorothy is unclear, except that we know that she had a piercing glance. It is no chance description, for he repeats the metaphor in line 149. He uses the word *wild* six times in the poem. In line 139 the words *wild ecstasies* seem to carry a meaning of those *dizzy raptures* of line 86; ones that mature in later life into *sober pleasure*.

123–124   It is hard to reconcile the idea expressed in these lines with some of the hardships inflicted by nature upon humanity which he describes in the ballads.

135–138   The paragraph is an extended blessing on his sister. Compare this sacramental act with that of the Ancient Mariner's blessing of the water snakes. It is interesting that Wordsworth's blessing employs almost entirely natural phenomena and the physical senses and does not imply divine grace, though he does describe his love for Dorothy as *holier love* (*Tintern Abbey*, line 156).

148–149   **where I no more can hear/Thy voice**   the poet's death. The final lines bring together past and present. The future will be a memorial to their joint lives.

In your final thoughts on this poem, as with all the poems, you may have discovered the ways in which these two great poets differ in their view of both man and nature. Both are Romantics in that the consciousness of man absorbed into nature is a Romantic discovery; but whereas Wordsworth was a Pantheist, who identified the forces within him as entirely natural and who acquired a tranquillity beyond the turmoil of the heart,

Coleridge was a Christian in an almost mystical sense, a restless spirit, a man of metaphysical imagination, a kind of mariner sailing the seas of abstract and religious thought alone in search of some kind of divine grace. Together they opened a new and fertile vein of thought and feeling which would endlessly inspire the imagination of the coming century.

Tintern Abbey by Francis Nicholson (watercolour).
(The Wordsworth Trust)

Interpretations

The Romantic tradition

The word *Romantic* is a relative rather than an absolute term, and no simple definition can be given for it. Romance (Romanticism) breaks through at different times and places and cultures in history. Resorting to the *Oxford English Dictionary* for a definition of the term does not help us, for there are over 70 different interpretations of the word. The word *Classic* is easier to define because its origins can be traced to ancient Greek culture. For that age, art and beauty were linked to truth and goodness, a means whereby mankind could be lifted *above* nature. Art was not merely representational, but it elevated and improved on nature, striving for a perfection of form, and for this the Greeks designed rules of proportion, symmetry and harmony almost mathematical in their precision.

Think of a Classical temple with its rows of columns and its pediment. It appears to rest calmly and solidly on the earth, self-contained and self-sufficient. Any added decoration would severely damage the symmetry of its lines. Think next of a Gothic cathedral and you will recognize that here there is a complexity of design, an irregularity of line, a restless and dynamic energy. This building is anything but calm, and seems not to be anchored to the earth at all. Whereas the Greek temple is a perfectly engineered box built as a sanctuary to protect a god, the Gothic church soars upwards to that Christian heaven to which the souls of men aspire. The arching windows, fretted roof and the spire itself symbolize the inner, spiritual man rather than the solid, material one. *Romantic* may be understood, therefore, as a progression of that philosophy which we call the medieval Gothic.

In literary terms the word was first applied to languages derived from Latin. The word is linked to Rome–Roman–Romance–Romantic. In the fourteenth century Chaucer would have understood the term as applying to tales of chivalry and

179

love written in the Romance languages – French and Italian. By the seventeenth century the word had come to mean unusual, imagined, strange or fantastic. Don Quixote was said to have his head filled with tales of old Romance. By the eighteenth century, the word had acquired the idea of something improbable, impractical, but really rather delightful. The essayist Joseph Addison, writing in the early newspaper *The Spectator* in 1712, speaks of the 'Pleasures of the Imagination':

> ...our Souls are at present delightfully lost and bewildered in a pleasing Seclusion, and we walk about like the enchanted Hero of Romance, who sees beautiful Castles, Woods and Meadows; and at the same time hears the warblings of Birds, and the purling of Streams; but upon the finishing of some secret Spell, the fantastic Scene breaks up, and the disconsolate Knight finds himself on a barren Heath, or in a solitary Desart.

There is a tone of amused parody here, of a dream world separate from the world of practical men, but words like *seclusion, spell, enchanted, castles, woods, meadows, the warbling of birds, the purling of streams* and *disconsolate knights* are the essence of Romanticism.

For the artists of the eighteenth century wedded to the neo-Classical tradition, Romance brought with it a sense of unease. The rules of good taste could not be infringed, because once overthrown the *civilizing* effects of art would be lost. Hence, gorges, mountains and precipices were things to avoid, for they diminished man. Picturesque they might be, but they threatened the order and sanity of society. Better to stick to neo-Classical buildings and good common sense. *The proper study of mankind was Man*, wrote the poet Alexander Pope. Man, not nature, was the centre and the measure of all things. Allow nature to prevail and all that mankind had carefully collected in the arts and sciences would collapse.

The Romantic tradition did not suddenly burst upon the world. First it became a topic of debate in European philosophical and artistic circles, where discussions began on the nature of beauty and the sublime; whether the imagination can be said to be objective or subjective; whether it is based on the memory or upon some other faculty, connected with inspiration, or intent, or able to create something entirely new? Can mind and body, reason and emotion be strictly held apart? Is the universe only a superior kind of machine? It was agreed that the Classical models were safe; their serenity and order had held good for centuries. But by the end of the eighteenth century, historical events placed this *order* in quite another light. It began to look stale and out of date.

By the 1790s a new philosophical language was taking hold. Words such as *genius*, *creative*, *inspiration* and *sublime* began to be used in connection with the imagination. Rousseau (1712–1778) argued that nature, like the inmates of the Bastille, had been kept too long in chains. Nature itself must be liberated. The very *opposite* of the rational view now became current. Allow man to return to nature and human ills would disappear. And it was the painters' attitude to landscape that led the movement for change. Wordsworth was born and bred in the Lake District, that most picturesque part of England, which had not been *discovered* in the aesthetic sense before the 1780s. Had he come from the mill towns of Yorkshire, the Romantic Movement in English poetry might have been delayed. Landscape now began to be *central* to the artist's creativity. In the same year that *Lyrical Ballads* was written, the painter William Turner was making his first major paintings of the Lake District. Nature was no longer perceived as a threat, but as a liberating and energizing power.

And so by 1798 a young woman like Dorothy Wordsworth could enthuse about the countryside of the Quantocks in words such as: *sea, woods wild as fancy ever painted, brooks clear and pebbly as in Cumberland, villages so romantic!*, and Coleridge could write a poem *On observing a Blossom on the First Day of February 1796* without blushing, for now action is suspended and the imagination set free. But, like the architects of the Gothic, the Romantic artist was searching for what can never really be known, something mystical and therefore outside the laws of reason. It follows that such art must be *experimental*. The only formal discipline that is acceptable is that which enables the artist to express a mood – *his* mood. Nor is he interested in some impersonal perfection but only in vehicles for his own imagination. There is also a geographical shift. The city is associated not with sophistication, but restriction and constraint. All true Romantics must seek the countryside.

Of course, in throwing overboard all the Classical models, the Romantic poet exposed himself to a number of risks. Romantic poetry can be inept if it is merely emotional self-indulgence. It is not enough to call it art because it expresses the poet's deepest and most sincere feelings. Art requires craftsmanship; indeed, that which seems most *natural* is often the most difficult to achieve. We shall see below how Wordsworth and Coleridge differed in their attitudes to the mechanics of poetry.

It is necessary here to say something about the Gothic tradition as it appeared at the end of the eighteenth century. The Gothic style is assumed to have begun with Horace Walpole's *The Castle of Otranto* (1864), the first tale of terror, but when the *real* Reign of Terror began in France, the taste for 'terror' in England suffered a temporary setback. In 1782 an important exhibition of paintings took place at the Royal Academy in London, over whose door were inscribed the words *Let no Man who is without Taste enter*. The exhibition featured pictures of idyllic rural scenes. Only one painting – *The Nightmare* by the artist Henry Fuseli – was different. It was a picture of a sleeping woman upon whose breast perched a hideous imp; through the bed curtains appeared the head of a white horse. The president of the Academy (Reynolds) uttered just one word of comment on seeing this picture – *Shocking!* Yet this work would become a Gothic icon, fuelling the imagination of many future artists including Coleridge. The effect of such paintings renewed interest in the darker side of the human psyche – dreams and madness, and what we now call the unconscious.

Both Wordsworth and Coleridge were analysts of the extreme mood and form of the Gothic. Wisely, they did not detach themselves completely from the neo-Classical style. Both wrote at their best in the blank-verse form brought to perfection by Milton. Wordsworth made the sonnet his particular field of expertise. But if we are looking for a formula for the Romantic style, we will look in vain. What links the two poets is not a common style but a common interest in a number of central ideas, all to be found in some form in *Lyrical Ballads*: a sense of mystery, conflict, interest in the extreme and abnormal, love, time, and the influence of the French Revolution.

A sense of mystery

Nature, including *human* nature, takes on an almost religious and mystical importance to the Romantic poet. A setting sun can appear like a prisoner staring through the bars of a dungeon, a thorn tree can seem like a small child; dancing twigs in the breeze become the workings of a child's or a mad woman's imagination, and can fascinate the poet's mind; each is equally important and strange when seen through the perspective of the Romantic imagination.

Conflict

To the Romantic, life always involves conflict against restrictive laws: a shepherd or an old woman is seen fighting against injustice; a convict or a political prisoner is portrayed as the victim of oppression; an old sailor strives to right the wrongs of the world by telling his story to a guest at a wedding; a dying Indian complains of the rules of the tribe.

Interest in the extreme and abnormal

Those at the extreme edges of society – beggars, the mad, the old, gipsies, the obsessive – are more interesting to the Romantic poet than people living in cities and leading humdrum lives. The Gothic mood is morbid yet opens the more dramatic psychological area of human experience. Nature, too, is most interesting in its more dramatic moods.

Love

As one of the most passionate and powerful of human emotions, love is constantly interesting to the Romantic poet. Lovers eloping from the restrictions of parental authority, sexual love, parental love, sibling love, love of country, love of nature – all figure prominently.

Time

Many poems in the collection are preoccupied with time. Perhaps the most obvious is *Lines Written a Few Miles above Tintern Abbey*. Think of the abbey as once a flawless medieval building which the hand of time has eroded. It is almost more beautiful when it has returned to nature. As the novelist Walter Scott wrote of Melrose Abbey: *If thou wouldst visit Melrose aright/Go visit her by the pale moonlight*. The important word here is *visit*. A pilgrimage must be made, and by moonlight, because at this moment, time makes the scene *sublime*.

Activity

Read through Coleridge's poem *The Nightingale* and Wordsworth's *Lines Written in Early Spring*. Consider the different moods. In what ways can these poems be said to be Romantic? Examine the different styles of language employed.

Discussion

You will have discovered in *The Nightingale* a magical atmosphere in which nature is more than a background; it is central to Coleridge's very being. He and his friends have learned a different lore whereby nature leads on to joy. The ruined castle and its overgrown grounds, where some gentle maid listens to the nightingales, is straight out of a Gothic romance; indeed, it is close to Addison's description on page 180. The reference to childhood recalls the Romantic interest in recovering lost innocence. Wordsworth's poem is less effusive, which seems in tune with what we know of his character. That sweet mood brings to him sad thoughts that griev'd my heart. Joy is modified to pleasure. Perhaps you can think of a reason why this is. Coleridge's style is rich and effusive while Wordsworth's is restrained, yet both poets see themselves as close to nature in the way that only a Romantic can, continually wishing to remind us of its life-giving powers.

The influence of the French Revolution

Romanticism was driven by the great artists who gave it direction in their personal lives, but it became generally acceptable only when the historical times were ready. Coleridge and Wordsworth were born at just the right moment. What turned the scales for them was the revolution in France. No young man or woman in the 1790s, just as in the 1930s, could avoid being swept into political allegiances. It seemed that, with the collapse of corrupt government in France, human misery would be abolished. The storming of the Bastille, even though it liberated only a handful of old men, was a potent symbol of freedom to the whole of Europe. To Wordsworth, Michael Beaupuy had died for the liberation of the common man. Although like most violent revolutions its character changed with the rise of a dictator, the Romantic genie was out of the bottle, and never again would Classical forms dominate the artistic world. Politically there were forlorn hopes for the writers of *Lyrical Ballads*, but to be Romantic was still heroic. Here was an opportunity for poets to make the case for freedom and equality. A lost paradise might still be recovered, and moreover presented in the real language of the common man. *Lyrical Ballads*, this small volume of poems, was nurtured in the spirit of rebellion.

The still, sad music of humanity

We have seen how the Romantics discovered nature as a source of joy and revelation, an alternative to the grim world of industrial cities; yet there is heartbreak, sadness and struggle against a dark universe in *Lyrical Ballads*. A female vagrant faces *disease, famine, agony and fear* (*The Female Vagrant*, line 128), ending her days without any *earthly friend*. A shepherd in *The Last of the Flock* feels that God has cursed him. The central character in *Lines left upon a Seat in a Yew-tree* is corroded by loneliness. A mad mother sings *many a sad and doleful song* (*The Mad Mother*, line 14) and feels that she will be *for ever sad* (line 90). Wordsworth turns *with a deep sadness* towards the convict's cell. The Mariner is *sad as sad could be* and the wedding guest becomes a *sadder and a wiser man*.

Wordsworth had no religious faith whatsoever at this time. He admits some kind of fall for humanity, but it is a fall from childlike innocence into the dreary, commonplace world of adult experience. He feels shame at continued human conflict, and his only consolations are nature, family and friends. His situation is almost more tragic than that of Coleridge, for a fall without hope of redemption seems bleak indeed.

In the Preface, Wordsworth tells us that he wishes *to keep my Reader in the company of flesh and blood* (Appendices, p. 233). By 1800 he had lost faith in political solutions, foreseeing further polarization of the classes: the effects of *gross and violent stimulants* taken to relieve the drudgery of labour or the *social vanity* of a wealthy middle class. In *Lines Written a Few Miles above Tintern Abbey* he fears that whether *in lonely rooms* or in *the din of towns and cities*, human suffering will increase to *a fever and a fret*. Few poems at this time possess that Classic calm, that spirit of acceptance of man's tragic destiny which the Greeks convey in their art. The ode seems to soften his sadness to a degree, but for the most part, the poems show us the world as *unintelligible* and being human as a *heavy weight* involving *hours of weariness*.

Activity

Examine Wordsworth's attitude to the state of human sadness, choosing three poems that present conflict and suffering. You may wish to explore the conflicts between hope/despair, justice /injustice, youth/age, sickness/health, good/evil or a combination of these. Confine your research to those *portraits* of men and women rather than the personal or reflective poems. What gives solace from the hardships of life?

Discussion

You have a wide range of poems from which to choose examples of conflict and suffering. In all the dramatic narratives we see and hear real people in distress. The poet restricts his view exclusively to the rural poor and, unlike poets of the previous century who had avoided such emotions, thereby reducing the human predicament to a series of set pieces and clichés, Wordsworth hides nothing of their suffering from us. He detests sentimentalizing poverty such as he found in Gray's *Elegy*. The horrors of destitution are starkly conveyed. The Indian and the vagrant woman have reached the lowest level of society; another winter may end Goody Blake; Simon Lee's dropsy means that he is too feeble to tend that little portion of subsistence land so dearly acquired; Martha Ray is locked into her monomania; the mad mother must seek shelter in woods; the convict is broken by disease and madness. Wordsworth records the suffering in graphic detail and tells us the causes – unemployment brought on by greedy landowners, the meagre wages of cottage industry, the lack of pensions for the old, the injustice of the Poor Laws and the insidious growth of industry which eats away at the poor man's liberty. He had placed his hopes in government reform, but war with France now seemed to indicate that a more tolerant society was a distant dream. Any remaining solace is strictly private and domestic: love of family, the charity of a neighbour, adherence to high moral values – honesty and self-discipline – and above all, the consolation of nature. Hence the destruction of the family is for Wordsworth the most savage cruelty of all, since for the poor, it is their *only* consolation.

Coleridge's attitude to suffering is different. He links the subject to the nature of evil itself. While Wordsworth is settling into a state of Stoic resignation in 1798, Coleridge ponders two different views of humanity. Is man essentially born good but ruined by his environment, or is he born sinful, predestined to evil unless redeemed by faith? Coleridge found it difficult to choose, for clearly there can be no compromise. In your reading of the two poems *The Nightingale* and *The Rime of the Ancyent Marinere* you will detect two different moods. The first shows us the power of the imagination as almost angelic. Nature is a paradise on earth. The second shows us mankind as cruel, guilty, and utterly dependent on God's grace. *The Foster-Mother's Tale* tells of the lost ideals of a boy, crushed by circumstances, driven to America, where he dies among *savage men* rather than endure the evils of sophistication. In his biography of Coleridge, Richard Holmes (*Early Visions*, Oxford University Press, 1982) suggests that the portrait was based on his elder brother Frank, who served with distinction in the Indian Army but, at the age of 22, contracted fever and shot himself in a delirium. *The Dungeon* also describes man's cruelty through a penal code that ignores the causes of crime and is based on revenge. How can this recurring pattern of suffering be explained except through original sin compounded by tyrannical government?

Writing to his brother George in March 1798, Coleridge declares *Of guilt I say nothing; but I believe most steadfastly in Original Sin; that from our mother's wombs our understandings are darkened* (*Letters*, vol. I, p. 396). Unlike Wordsworth, whose political hopes were collapsing, Coleridge had always distrusted political as well as religious dogma. He thought Godwin's atheism and radicalism odious. On the first occasion they met, he found that Godwin *talked sophisms in jejune language* (*Letters*, vol. I, p. 215). Passionate about social justice, Coleridge insists that man can only understand himself through God, not God through man. Of such truth he had lectured in Bristol in 1795:

It is not enough, that we have swallowed it – the Heart should have fed upon the truth as insects on a Leaf – till it be tinged with the colour, and shew its food in every the minutest fibre.

(Letters, vol. I, p. 115)

Thus, if man is miserable it is through his own selfishness; nevertheless, he shares in the divine nature of a merciful God through Christ and may find redemption, if not in this world, then in the next.

In your study of *The Rime of the Ancyent Marinere* you may discover something of an old morality tale in which angels and daemons struggle for power over the Mariner's soul. These daemons are male and female, a reminder of Adam and Eve whose progeny we are. Since the Fall, sin has been multiplied, locking humanity inside a dungeon of the baser self. In a notebook, Coleridge speaks of these daemons of his age as Mammon (greed for money), *the fiend Hag Anxiety*, the terrors of superstition and sexual depravity – *gloomy Daemons both that love the Dark*. It is therefore impossible to study Coleridge's poetry as something separate from his faith; without some concept of a Fall, his poetry is unintelligible. A dreamlike quality in his work speaks of another world beyond the earthly. If Wordsworth speaks of flesh and blood, Coleridge always looks beyond it.

Activity

Study the character of the Ancient Mariner. Why is the killing of the Albatross so important and why, at first, does the Mariner seem unconcerned about his action? Distinguish between the universe and the Mariner himself. What alienates him from his environment? What finally connects him? Compare your *past* view of him with your *final* view.

Discussion

The whole weight of the poem rests upon an act of murder. The killing of a bird may seem too slight a thing to merit the suffering that ensues, but the Albatross is not just a physical organism. Coleridge was not a conservationist in the modern sense, nor should we attach to him the Victorian sentimentality of all things bright and beautiful. The really important thing is that the murder is committed by one who is ignorant of its moral implications. He represents fallen humanity which lives in a mist. Only by suffering is conscience aroused; till then, mankind is in hell. Coleridge believed that man is, in part, possessed by daemons – a lack of compassion through a lack of thought – and these are of his own making. Selfishness destroys kinship between humanity and the universe, and thus the Mariner becomes increasingly isolated. Finally, only he survives, locked inside a dungeon of his own creation. The sailors are not absolved from sin for they are motivated only by superstition, but they are eventually redeemed, and released into death. Strangely, it is through an evil act that the Mariner recognizes his sin; yet this is the vital religious truth in the poem. To understand, man must first forget and then remember; to love, he must first lose and then win back. Only by pain and fall will he know himself and gain redemption. His homecoming is a return to God and the community by which he is healed. Finally, he acquires humility, but not peace. Only death can bring that. For the sake of others he must repeat every detail of his ordeal. As a non-believer Wordsworth offers no such divine healing. Whereas Coleridge believes in prayer to a transcendental power, Wordsworth takes refuge in the powers within humanity itself.

Some discussion of the theme of childhood is necessary here because it figures prominently in at least four of the poems – *The Nightingale, The Idiot Boy, Anecdote for Fathers* and *We Are Seven*. These deal with innocence, a state in which the imagination is actively combined with the absence of anxiety. Yet the state is permanently under threat from adult cynicism and selfishness. All the children in *Lyrical Ballads* live symbiotically with nature – a feast of revelation and vibrant possibilities. In *The Nightingale*, a distressed child is comforted by a glimpse of the moon; the idiot boy is drunk with pleasure at being allowed to spend the night wandering the woods on his pony *careless as if nothing were* (line 360). In *Anecdote for Fathers* Wordsworth asks how a five-year-old can deal with memory, a rather pointless exercise since the child's experience of time is non-existent. Wisely, the child changes the subject rather than give a considered reply, and the poet is made to look foolish. A different aspect of childhood is explored in *We Are Seven*. The girl is convinced that the family is undivided by death because death for her, like time for Edward, is meaningless. Her dead siblings are merely sleeping and so close that she and her brother play around their graves and talk to them.

Coleridge believed that Wordsworth was in danger of overestimating the significance of childhood, seeing too many hidden meanings in childish prattle (see Notes, p. 152). However, both poets insist that a healthy childhood is essential to the growth of the moral sense. Both idealize the maternal relationship, believing that the child expands its own capacity for love through the love of its mother. Deep attachment to home and place is the true patriotism. This view of childhood was quite new in society and the sense of its sacredness in most people's minds today is partly due to the way that the Romantics taught us to think and feel.

Activity

Make a close study of *The Idiot Boy*, a poem in which Wordsworth explores the maternal relationship. The fact that it gave him so much pleasure to write shows that he was fascinated by this state of innocent reciprocal love. Compare the poem with one other poem which deals with a mother and child. Consider the way Wordsworth attempts to capture the language of everyday speech in order to convey a sense of actuality.

Discussion

In *Tintern Abbey* Wordsworth tells us that adulthood is a decline from an exciting state of *aching joy* (line 85) to *dizzy rapture* (line 86) and to the *dreary intercourse of daily life* (line 132). The idiot boy still lives in a dream world. So powerful is it that even Betty recovers its rapture when she finds Johnny safe. Betty's sacrifice of her treasured son for the sake of Susan reveals that other vital love, of one's neighbour. The story ends in blissful reunion; even the pony has his share of glory. There is heroism in failure, for Johnny *did his best*. The father is scarcely mentioned, and in other poems fatherhood is criticized. The partners of both Martha Ray and the mad mother have abandoned them. Wordsworth would address this imbalance in the second edition of *Lyrical Ballads* in his poem *Michael*, a moving study of fatherhood.

In examining the language you will have discovered that, in Wordsworth's use of the ballad form, narrative is always linked to character and feeling. Here is what Wordsworth calls *the real language of men*, words and phrases suited to a simple countrywoman's life. Coleridge criticizes Wordsworth for being too particular, but in fact, when Betty finds her son and the poem reaches its climax, she represents that universal place in the heart, the *primal sympathy* which redeems humanity from moral ruin. Wordsworth believes such feelings are the source of those *elevated thoughts, a sense sublime./Of something far more deeply interfused/Whose dwelling is the light of setting suns* (*Tintern Abbey*, lines 96–98).

In comparing the two writers' attitudes to the human condition, do not polarize their views. There *are* fundamental differences, which will be examined further below, but they are as one mind in their wish to restore humanity to a closer relationship with nature. Notice that Wordsworth uses the words *the still, sad music of humanity*. The word *still* implies that sadness seems destined to be repeated endlessly, but if the sadness is *still*, it is also *music*. Human love and endurance in the face of adversity have, for Wordsworth, a music of their own, as for Romantic composers such as Beethoven and Chopin. There is heroism among ordinary human beings. Even a child can look beyond death. If in his later poetry an optimism and tenderness appear, finally to be resolved in his becoming a Christian, we must recognize that, in *Lyrical Ballads*, Wordsworth inclines more towards suffering. The years ahead would bring him fame but also grief, and the deaths of his brother at sea in 1805 and three of his five children would be hard to bear. But Wordsworth would never acquire anything like Coleridge's passionate religious faith. Coleridge was to live for almost twenty years separated from his wife and children, yet he would become one of England's most seminal literary critics. As a philosopher, his full status has yet to be assessed (see the comment by John Stuart Mill in Interpretations, p. 217). He would never recover from his addiction to opium – proof in his own life of his conviction that earthly existence is always plagued by daemons of one kind or another.

Wordsworth's Preface of 1800

Before embarking on what is a complex discussion of the Preface in conjunction with Coleridge's views (*Biographia Literaria* 1815–1817) it will be useful to sketch the events between the two editions of *Lyrical Ballads* of which the Preface is a singular part.

Coleridge prolonged his tour of Germany until June 1799. Meanwhile, the Wordsworths had returned to the Lake District. Coleridge's first visit there in October filled him with rapture and Wordsworth pressed him to move north. Coleridge had obligations as a journalist with *The Morning Post*, where he was involved in political controversy, even making friends with Godwin who later claimed that Coleridge's conversation had forced him to reconsider his atheism! However, the beauty of the Lakes was so bewitching that in June 1800 Coleridge 'burned his boats' behind him, investing heavily in Wordsworth's friendship. In many ways it was to be a tragic mistake.

After an initially disappointing reception, the first edition of *Lyrical Ballads* became a talking point in literary circles. Wordsworth was keen to publish a second edition in two volumes, to include more of his own poems. Coleridge agreed to edit these in addition to finishing his Gothic poem *Christabel* and continuing his work as a freelance journalist. From an initial position of weakness, Wordsworth now came to dominate the terms of their partnership, announcing that he wished to exclude the *Ancyent Marinere* from the new edition on the grounds that it jarred with his rural tales:

> The poem of my Friend has indeed great defects; first, that the principal person has no distinct character, either in his profession as a Mariner, or as a human being who having been long under the control of supernatural impressions might be supposed himself to partake of something supernatural: secondly, that he does not act, but is continually acted upon: thirdly, that the events having no necessary connection do not produce each other; and lastly, that the imagery is somewhat too laboriously accumulated...the metre itself is unfit for long poems.

> (*Letters*, vol. I, pp. 544–5)

Coleridge was deeply hurt by this literary demolition of the poem, seeing it as an attack on his artistic integrity, and it seems astonishing that Wordsworth should have failed to recognize the poem's unique power and originality. Nor was this the only blow. Wordsworth also refused to include *Christabel* on the grounds that medieval balladry was discordant with the theme of the new book. The *Marinere* was reprieved, but only after Coleridge had made 71 changes and agreed to place it second to last in the collection. Wordsworth's *Michael* replaced *Christabel*. The edition triumphantly ended with *Lines Written a Few Miles above Tintern Abbey*. Thus, the second volume, containing 41 of Wordsworth's new poems, placed the greater emphasis on himself, Coleridge meekly agreeing that the title should be *Lyrical Ballads with other Poems in two volumes by W. Wordsworth*. As he wrote to a friend: *He is a great, a true Poet – I am only a kind of Metaphysician. He has even now sent off the last sheet of a second Volume of his* Lyrical Ballads (*Letters*, vol. I, p. 658). As Coleridge's biographer Richard Holmes writes: *the possessive pronoun said it all* (*Early Visions*, p. 286).

Coleridge's two poems, with their daemonic machinery, their

daylight witchery, haunting rhythms and psychological insights, might have unbalanced the book, but this division of the natural and supernatural had been the agreed form of the collection. Wordsworth's dismissal was to help to derail Coleridge's self-confidence as a poet. He began to withdraw into his obscure books, cramming his notebooks with details of incessant walking tours over the fells and, with declining health in the damp climate, resorting more and more to opium. In the months and years ahead he would mourn the loss of his poetic powers and question his partnership with Wordsworth.

You will find that the Preface as printed in the Appendices is that of 1800. An insertion of Wordsworth's made in 1802 and Chapter XIV from Coleridge's *Biographia Literaria* follow. In this section the main body of Wordsworth's poetic theory will be discussed in connection with that of Coleridge, though not restricted to a single chapter in *Biographia Literaria*. Reference will also be made to Chapters XIII–XVIII (the edition referred to is a verbatim print of the first edition published by Bell & Son in London, 1898).

In reading the Preface you may feel that, noble as the sentiments are, it is not an objective treatise on poetry or critical theory. Possibly it arose from two of Wordsworth's strong dislikes: eighteenth-century notions of poetry as *the dress of thought* (it was absurd to look for a thought and then clothe it in some suitable attire) and his aversion to subjects and styles suited only to cultivated readers. Yet he is sensitive to criticism from these readers, anxious to assure them that his tales are built on wide-ranging and deeply-held views not just on poetry, but on society itself. His dogmatic tone suggests that the defence has assumed more than the casual motive he admits – that his friends had urged him to write it. He said in later life that *he did not care a straw about it*, but his continued tinkering with it over the next 15 years contradicts this. Clearly he wanted to leave behind a comprehensive and sublime theory of poetry. Faulty as it is, the work has entered the popular understanding of Romanticism and has left an indelible mark on later writers.

To summarize some of the major features in the first stages of the argument.

First, Wordsworth defines poetry in *Lyrical Ballads* as *fitting to metrical arrangement a selection of the real language of men in a state of vivid sensation, that sort of pleasure and that quantity of pleasure may be imparted, which a Poet may rationally endeavour to impart* (Appendices, p. 227). He makes an early reference to Coleridge's contribution, adding that their opinions on poetry *almost entirely coincided.* He forbears to discuss whether current fashions in taste are either *healthy or depraved*, preferring to describe his own motives based on his own compositions. He explains his focus on common life as based on his belief that *the essential passions of the heart find a better soil in which they can attain their maturity, are less under restraint, and speak a plainer and more emphatic language* (Appendices, p. 229). This greater simplicity is more easily understood, more lasting and closer to the beautiful and permanent forms of nature. It is not distorted by *social vanity* because rural occupations deal with repeated experience and are therefore more *philosophical*. Wordsworth does not tell us what this word means. He proceeds to his famous definition of good poetry: *all good poetry is the spontaneous overflow of powerful feelings; but though this be true, Poems to which any value can be attached, were never produced on any variety of subjects but by a man who being possessed of more than usual organic sensibility, had also thought long and deeply* (Appendices, p. 230).

It is important to make it clear that Wordsworth does *not* say – as is often quoted – that poetry is *only* feeling. However, the thrust of his argument throughout is always to show feeling – the language of the heart – as more important than thinking. The very tone of this first part suggests a man who has made up his mind on the subject largely on the basis of his own practical experience rather than on any objective consideration. He seems slightly annoyed that we may question his motives.

Coleridge's response, written some 15 years later, is part of a larger work on philosophy and the views expressed are consistent with a large-scale and integrated concept of imagination. In

Chapter XIV of *Bigraphia Literaria*, Coleridge denies that he had concurred with Wordsworth's views but had indeed *objected to them as erroneous in principle, and as contradictory (in appearance at least) both to other parts of the same preface and to the author's own practice* (Appendices, p. 254). Pleasure may result from poetry, he asserts, but it is not itself the immediate end: pleasure may be the immediate purpose; and though truth, either moral or intellectual, ought to be the ultimate end, yet this will distinguish the character of the author, not the class to which the work belongs (Appendices, p. 256).

At once we discover a very different kind of reasoning. Coleridge uses language in a more analytical way. He gives his own definition of a poem as *that species of composition, which is opposed to works of science, by proposing for its immediate object pleasure, not truth; and from all other species (having this object in common with it) it is discriminated by proposing to itself such delight from the whole, as is compatible with a distinct gratification from each component part...all in their proportion harmonising with, and supporting the purpose and known influences of metrical arrangement* (Appendices, pp. 256–7). He argues that no individual lines should distort the harmony of the whole. It is the mind's *journey* through the poem that gives pleasure, not the attainment of any specific goal. Here is Coleridge's concept of the organic form of a poem – a union of thought, feeling and structure which has no *single* object, least of all one restricting it to any social or intellectual class or particular morality, but a multiplicity of objects all actively engaged with each other.

Wordsworth's argument is a moral and aesthetic complex. He insists that poetry should have *a worthy purpose* – later he tells us what social conditions he opposes. Feeling – *great and simple affections of our nature* – is paramount. He specifies the maternal affection as one of the most important emotions, something explored widely in *Lyrical Ballads*. What distinguishes his poetry from his contemporaries is *our feelings and ideas are associated in a state of excitement...the feeling therein developed gives importance to the action and situation and not the action and situation to the feeling*. Such an emphasis on feeling falls short of Coleridge's comprehensive though more complex definition of the imagination.

You will find Coleridge's definition of imagination in the conclusion to Chapter XIII. It is almost impossible to summarize, but basically Coleridge divides imagination into two kinds: primary and secondary imagination.

Primary imagination is basic to every human being (in fact, Coleridge goes so far as to indicate that it is the primary condition of consciousness itself), particularly perceptible in childhood and what we would now call the sub-conscious mind.

Secondary imagination is the same in kind but is the special province of the artist, the greatest being able to *control* the primary power by the *will*, creating something that is not merely dependent on the laws of association but entirely *original*.

In addition to imagination there is what Coleridge calls the *Fancy*. This is dependent on the memory. It is vital to the artist but is of a lesser kind than secondary imagination. Any moderately talented person would be able to write a poem out of the Fancy, but it is not poetry in the highest sense. Clearly, Wordsworth's continued emphasis on feeling as diffused through the memory as the heart of poetry is very different from Coleridge's understanding of imagination. In his preoccupation with moral teaching, Wordsworth looks back to the eighteenth century just as his view of nature is close to eighteenth-century deism[4]. Imagination, as Coleridge understands it, is more modern, and is a word Wordsworth almost never uses.

---

[4] Deism is the belief that the individual can only discover truth through reason and nature without resort to religion or revelation.

In the next part of the Preface Wordsworth doggedly continues to argue that he wishes to combat certain tendencies in modern society: *a multitude of causes unknown to former times are now acting with a combined force to blunt the discriminating powers of the mind, and unfitting it for all voluntary exertion to reduce it to a state of almost savage torpor. The most effective of these causes are the great national events which are daily taking place, and the increasing accumulation of men in cities, where the uniformity of their occupations produces a craving for extraordinary incident which the rapid communication of intelligence hourly gratifies* (Appendices, p. 232). This statement applies equally to our own society. Wordsworth is justly condemning the increasing pace of life as destroying those conditions in which any calm study of our primary values is possible. It underlines his conviction that poetry should have a moral purpose and it is to this very sentiment that readers after Charles Darwin would turn as consolation for lost faith. But noble as this view is, it does not seem to be an adequate principle on which to base a theory of poetry.

Coleridge's definition at the end of Chapter XIV looks much more substantial. Look at the important paragraph on page 258 that begins '*My own conclusions on the nature of poetry...*'. Such a comprehensive description – based on Coleridge's idea of the ideal poet, Shakespeare – needs little comment except to say that Wordsworth's rather plodding exegesis seems modest in comparison. Coleridge's view that a great poet must *always* be a great philosopher is questionable. Wordsworth is no philosopher, yet he is undoubtedly a great poet, though not a poet in the same mould as Shakespeare. If he can be likened to any English *species* of poet it might be Milton, though Wordsworth spurns that huge mythological and religious structure essential to epic poetry relying on autobiography – the Romantic's dilemma in throwing aside the Classical tradition.

The 'real language of men'

In the 1802 Preface, Wordsworth deals with language as *a selection of the language really spoken by men* and his preference for country life as providing language closer to poetry (*Appendices*, p. 244). In Chapter XVII of the *Biographia Literaria*, Coleridge argues that the language in his rural tales is by no means taken from low and rustic life. Such tales are to be found in every state of life, both town and country. The language is neither plain nor emphatic; nor does it spring from a finer soil. He is critical of *The Idiot Boy*, describing it as *an impersonation of an instinct abandoned by judgement*. Morbid images of the boy's insanity and the mother's folly are, for Coleridge, nothing more than *a laughable burlesque on the blindness of anile dotage*. He condemns the language of the sea-captain in *The Thorn* as banal.

The word that Coleridge finds objectionable is *real*. *Everyman's language has, first its individuality; secondly, the common properties of the class to which he belongs; and thirdly, words and phrases of universal use* (*BL*, Ch. XVII, p. 170). All are equally real. Take out the provincialisms and grossness from rustic language and it will not differ from the common language of any man *except as far as the notions which the rustic has to convey are fewer and more indiscriminate*. Wordsworth's rustic differs markedly from the common peasant. For *real*, he means *ordinary*. *Omit the peculiarities of each, and the result of course must be common to all* (*BL*, Ch. XVII, p. 171). The variables of every town and village make any concept of *real language* absurd. Take, for instance, the opening stanza of *The Last of the Flock*; no rustic would use repeated inversions. Equally, the stanza from *The Thorn* beginning *At all times of day and night/This wretched woman thither goes* is as unlike ordinary – or indeed rustic – language as could possibly be – the reason, perhaps, why it is so beautiful. Coleridge adds wryly: *I reflect with delight, how little a mere theory, though of his own workmanship, interferes with the processes of genuine imagination in a man of true poetic genius* (*BL*, Ch. XVIII, p. 173).

Prose and poetry

Wordsworth's dislike of poetic diction as distinct from common language stems from his fear that language will become dissociated from feeling. Implicit in his thoughts about language is his fear that it can become conceptualized like science. Concepts are for men like Coleridge. Wordsworth can accept no metaphysic of imagination, nor theory based on abstract or speculative reasoning. For Coleridge, imagination has to be considered in the light of first principles and problems of ultimate reality. Wordsworth is interested only in the *function* of imagination as he employs it in *his own* poetry. For him, language is a kind of incarnation. No one would question this profound truth. That there can be one language for art and another for nature, as Gray had expressed, is clearly wrong, but Wordsworth's refusal to admit *any* separation of language and life – that *we murder to dissect* – lies behind his rather confused argument that there is no essential difference between prose and poetry.

For Wordsworth, prose and poetry are essentially alike because they are the same media and deal with human experience. It is only the addition of metre that is different. This invites the question of why Wordsworth chooses to write in verse at all, to which he replies that although metre constitutes *only a small part of the pleasure given* in poetic form, one cannot merely extract a *part* of poetry. It all comes in the same package, so to speak. If the end of poetry is pleasure, it is essential to use the widest range of imagery and metaphor to produce that pleasure. To create excitement and a heightened sense of feeling, images must be powerful. Metre helps to restrain this exuberance. Wordsworth argues that Shakespeare never goes beyond the bounds of taste when dealing with violent subjects – a statement open to dispute. He sees no contradiction here. Coleridge argues that written prose differs from ordinary conversation in proportion as prose differs from poetry. That there are parts of poems that are prose-like and parts of prose that are poetic is undeniable, but a poem is built in such a way that *every word is organically part of the whole*. In a great poem we find not only the best words in the best order, but the *only* words in that order, which is not something that can be said for prose. *Things identical must be convertible* (BL, Ch. XVIII, p. 176), and prose and poetry are clearly not. As for metre, Coleridge argues that it should act in an unseen way, as wine animates a conversation, a stimulant to the attention and a pleasure in itself unique to poetry. If passion is a vital part of poetry and every passion has its pulse, so every poem has its own metre and this, as everything else in the poem, must be in harmony with the poet's own voice and character.

Emotion recollected in tranquillity

In the next stage of his treatise, Wordsworth describes the creative process as *emotion recollected in tranquillity*. In recalling past emotions, the mind of the poet is generally in a state of enjoyment. The poet finds pleasure in tempering the joys or pains of past experience through the effort of finding graceful forms of language, rhyme and metre. Again, this is a personal view. Can it be said that the poet *always* creates in a state of pleasure? The process may be painful, since it requires empathy with the subject and often an exhausting re-examination of the initial thoughts or feelings. Neither can Coleridge accept that poetry depends solely on memory. For him, memory is dependent on the laws of association whereas imagination is an *original* power (see BL, Ch. XIII).

In the final stage of the 1800 Preface, Wordsworth asks his reader to decide *by his own feelings genuinely, and not by reflection upon what will probably be the judgement of others* (Appendices, p. 242). This smacks slightly of desperation. It is sound advice if one reads poetry purely for pleasure, but if one is looking for a theory of what constitutes the highest quality of a poem, the pleasure principle is inadequate. Wordsworth urges his readers to temper their judgement with a spirit of continued improvement of their taste. He refers yet again to Reynolds: *an accurate taste in Poetry and in all the other arts, as Sir Joshua Reynolds has observed, is an acquired talent, which can only be produced by thought and a long continued intercourse with the best models of composition* (Appendices, pp. 242–3). This seems contrary to the spirit of the Preface where Wordsworth has argued for the ordinary reader and it raises the thorny question: *What is taste?* In an age of relative taste like ours, when what is enjoyable to one is detestable to another, is it possible to define 'taste'? Finally, Wordsworth appeals to his readers to judge for themselves.

Wordsworth's friends had warned him that there would be strong reactions to the Preface, but it made little impression on the public. Undaunted, Wordsworth decided that, with yet another edition, he would wrestle again with his theory. In 1802 he inserted a further section. This contains a long and interesting definition of the poet:

> He is a man speaking to men: a man, it is true, endued with more lively sensibility, more enthusiasm and tenderness, who has a greater knowledge of human nature, and a more comprehensive soul than are supposed to be common among mankind; a man pleased with his own passions and volitions, and who rejoices more than other men in the spirit of life that is in him...To these qualities he has added a disposition to be affected more than other men by absent things as if they were present; an ability of conjuring up in himself passions, which are indeed far from being the same as those produced by real events...he has acquired a greater readiness and power in expressing what he thinks and feels, and especially those thoughts and feelings which, by his own choice, or from the structure of his own mind, arise in him without immediate external excitement.

> (Appendices, pp. 245–6)

This is more carefully worded than his earlier definition but continues to stress the passions and sympathies of the poet. Wordsworth allows that these may be distanced from reality. He states that however exalted the poet's feelings, they are but shadows *of real and substantial action and suffering*. The poet is a *translator* of experience, a man speaking to men, closer than any other person in being able to communicate these feelings. He sees the poet's task as mediating between real life and art and in some way acting as a kind of maturing process through meditation and memory, sacredly transmitting his experiences and speaking words of consolation to suffering humanity. He refers to Aristotle: *Aristotle, I have been told, hath said, that Poetry is the most philosophic of all writing: it is so: its object is truth, not individual and local, but general and operative; not standing upon external testimony, but carried alive into the heart by passion* (Appendices, p. 247) – but Aristotle sees all art as a *making*, not a *translating* process. Coleridge's theory is closer to Aristotle's in seeing poetry as an *active* process based on a reconciliation of opposites. Thought and feeling wrestle with each other until they find rest in form. Coleridge is thinking in the tradition of Renaissance Platonism in seeing the artist creating a *better* world: *just as the calm sea to us appears level, though it be indeed only a part of a Globe...what the Globe is in Geography,* miniaturing *in order to manifest the truth, such is a poem to that image of God* (*Unpublished Letters of Samuel Taylor Coleridge*, ed. E.L. Griggs, 2 vols, Constable, 1932, vol. II, p. 619). Wordsworth is unhappy about this conscious *making* – though no poet worked harder on the 'nuts and bolts' of verse – but for him, poetry comes through a natural process of meditation and recollection. As he wrote in a letter of 1814 on the teaching of children about the universe: *There is nothing in the course of the religious education as adopted in this country...that appears to me so injurious as perpetually talking about making by God...for heaven's sake, in your religious talk with children, say as little as possible about* making (*The Letters of William and Dorothy Wordsworth*, ed. E. de Selincourt, 6 vols, Oxford, 1935–1939, vol. III: 1811–1820, p. 619).

The 1802 insertion is not without its noble sentiments expressed in powerful and moving language – no doubt why it appealed strongly to later poets. The following passage is finely expressed and Coleridge would have approved of this elevated view of the poet's role:

> The Man of Science seeks truth as a remote and unknown benefactor; he cherishes and loves it in his solitude: the Poet, singing a song in which all human beings join with him, rejoices in the presence of truth as our visible friend and hourly companion. Poetry is the breath and finer spirit of all knowledge; it is the impassioned expression which is in the countenance of all Science...He [the Poet] is the rock of defence of human nature; an upholder and preserver, carrying everywhere with him relationship and love. In spite of difference of soil and climate, of language and manners, of laws and customs, in spite of things silently gone out of mind and things violently destroyed, the Poet binds together by passion and knowledge the vast empire of human society...

(Appendices, p. 249)

We end this section of Interpretations with two activities.

Activity
How well do you think Wordsworth makes his case for the role of the poet? Compare his theory with your reading of Coleridge's views in Chapter XIV of his *Biographia Literaria* and what you have learned from this section. How far do you think Coleridge is correct in his view that any definition of poetry is virtually the same as asking: what is a poet?

Discussion
Wordsworth makes a good case for his *own* poetry but not for *all* poetry. You may have summarized his principles as:

- Poetry should not be exclusive but written as a man speaking to men.
- Language should be a selection of the *real language of men*.

- It is the duty of the poet to convey real experiences as accurately as possible and these experiences are best seen in country life.
- Poetry is a spontaneous overflow of powerful feelings.
- There is no essential difference between prose and poetry.
- The process of writing poetry is to recollect past experience in a state of tranquillity.
- The poet has a more comprehensive soul than other men.

Make your own judgements on the validity of Wordsworth's argument, but keep in mind that Coleridge and Wordsworth argue from different premises and perspectives. Coleridge is attempting to establish a rational principle rather than pass judgement on what has been written by himself or others. He argues that the poetic genius is instinctive – if it depended only on rules it would cease to be poetry – but poetry is also *made*. The imagination itself is the rule. He observes that were Wordsworth to abide strictly by his own theory, two-thirds of his poetry would be erased. Wordsworth is an overt moralizer. He wants to be seen as a teacher, to make sense of the world around him. The main weight of his argument rests on the importance of feeling and the poetic memory; thus his handling of abstract argument is unclear. He refuses to separate poetry from life, yet art and life are not the same.

Activity

Choose two or three poems that employ what Wordsworth means by the real *language of men*. How far does he demonstrate in these poems the theory which he puts forward in his Preface, and how successful are they as poems?

Discussion

A case can be made for some of his rural portraits, but not all. They can be read and enjoyed by ordinary people and Wordsworth's attempt to use colloquial language is new in literature, but he spoils some poems by including mundane details. It may be unfair to judge him harshly in what he designed as an experiment, but the fact that he puts forward a theory implies that he expects to be judged by the principles of theoretical analysis.

Nature and mysticism

> In youth and early manhood the mind and nature are, as it were, two rival artists...For a while the mind seems to have the better in the contest, and makes of Nature what it likes, takes her lichens and weather-stains for types and printer's ink, and prints maps and facsimiles of Arabic and Sanscrit MSS, on her rocks; composes country dances on her moonshiny ripples, fandangos on her waves, and waltzes on her eddy-pools, transforms her summer gales into harps and harpers, lovers' sighs and sighing lovers, and her winter blasts into Pindaric Odes, Christabels, and Ancient Mariners set to music by Beethoven...But alas! alas! that Nature is a wary wily long-breathed old witch, tough lived as a turtle and divisible as the polyp...She is sure to get the better of Lady *Mind* in the long run...

> (*Letters of Samuel Taylor Coleridge*, ed. E.H. Coleridge, 2 vols, 1895, vol. II, pp. 742–3)

So wrote Coleridge in 1825. Its sentiment seems a long way from his rapturous view of nature in 1798. Or is it? Although in *The Nightingale* the magical power of nature lifts his heart, it wears a different face in *The Rime of the Ancyent Marinere* where Nature slaughters innocent and wicked alike and will roast a man alive. It is hard to see how Wordsworth's faith in nature can apply to the suffering Mariner or the dying Indian. What, then, do the Romantics see in nature that is so special?

The answer is complex, but we may approach it by looking at some of the different ways these two poets present the theme. Look first at the following lines: *To her fair works did nature link/The human soul that through me ran* (*Lines Written in Early Spring*, lines 5–6), and *Let nature be your teacher* (*The Tables Turned*, line 16). Wordsworth links nature to himself almost physically. His body *breathes* its energy as *every flower/Enjoys the air it breathes* (*Lines Written in Early Spring*, lines 11–12). In the last lines of *The Tables Turned* he mentions *a heart/That watches and receives*. Examine the verbs here – *breathing, watching, receiving, listening* – all passive activities. Nature seems eager to please man, conveying *a thrill of pleasure*, charming his ear with *a thousand blended notes* or refreshing him with *the breezy air*. Only wait in a mood of *wise passiveness* and nature teaches us everything worth learning, including morality. Books only get in the way. Wordsworth employs harsh words about man – *lament, meddling, murder, dissect*. In *Expostulation and Reply*, man is *forlorn and blind*. In *Tintern Abbey*, nature is *the nurse,/The guide, the guardian of my heart, and soul/Of all my moral being* (lines 110–112). Wordsworth puts *all* his faith in nature. But in what way is nature a nurse? He answers: nature gives *healing thoughts* and *tender joy*. But can there be any direct link with what is a vast, impersonal force unrelated to morality? Surely it is the *beauty* of nature that conveys joy and consolation, and how can beauty be a part of nature when it is clearly an attribute of mind? For Wordsworth, nature, not God, is his refuge; in fact, he calls himself *a worshipper of Nature* (*Tintern Abbey*, line 153). This is Pantheism. Nature is a substitute for God.

Coleridge takes a different view. For him, Pantheism is atheism. No one adores the beauty of nature more than he, but in climbing a mountain he feels his soul soaring up to his Creator. His soul yearns to identify with the transcendental. Wordsworth finds this side of Coleridge self-indulgent, *strained and unnatural*. For him the *act* of climbing Snowdon, the struggle and then the isolation of it all, is the pleasure. When he sees the moon emerging from a cloud over Snowdon he sees a symbol of something *That broods/Over the dark abyss* (*The Prelude*, Book XIV, lines 71–72). Man and his world are the dark abyss. To have climbed a great mountain is not to be transfigured but to escape the abyss, to be self-sufficient, even heroic, as his old beggars, vagrants and mad women are heroic, finding truth not outside but within themselves. Coleridge is disturbed by this inwardness. Though he admires Wordsworth's strength of purpose, he seems a mere spectator. In 1802 he wrote of

Wordsworth, *he appears to me to have hurtfully segregated and isolated his Being* (*Letters*, vol. II, pp. 830–1). He felt Wordsworth to be *all male. It is good for him to be alone.* There did not seem to be any femininity in his nature – a fault in a poet. In dividing their skills it was Coleridge who was to supply the supernatural – all moonlight – and Wordsworth who was to present things of everyday.

Look at Coleridge's poem *The Nightingale.* It shows the enthusiasm of a *young* man. Wordsworth seems never to have been young in the same way, *surrendering his whole spirit* (line 29). Words such as *glimmer, glitter, glistening, tipsy* and *airy* convey euphoria. The nightingale's song is *delicious* – a word Wordsworth would never have used. In this paradisal infinity Coleridge loses himself, feeling *I am nothing.* Wordsworth finds himself in beauty, feeling *I am everything.* The ego becomes sublime; fear and pain are subsumed, healed and fortified.

A perfect example of Wordsworth's transmission of experience is to be found in his poem '*I wandered lonely as a Cloud*', which he *transposed* largely from Dorothy's journal. Dorothy's description is full of spontaneous emotion, but in the finished poem Wordsworth has thrown a colouring of quietness over it – a state of recollection. (Sandra Anstey discusses this poem in the Oxford Student Texts edition of *William Wordsworth: Selected Poems*, Oxford University Press, pp. 141–2.) Coleridge believed that Wordsworth had placed too much faith in nature, and that mind should rule over the senses. Neither can he accept that nature is a moral teacher, for nature is not always ennobling. Are Goody Blake's or Simon Lee's lives of meagre subsistence noble? For Coleridge, nature strives to become *mind*; for Wordsworth, nature strives to become *man.* A primrose *enjoys the air it breathes*, a bird feels *pleasure*, an old thorn is a suffering old man. For Coleridge, the *beauty* of nature can heal *the wandering and distempered child* (*The Dungeon*, line 21), but it is nature in mild and sweet moods, not nature in the raw.

Wordsworth was convinced that nature leads directly to joy

and love, but an absolute chasm exists between mind and nature. Coleridge believed nature to be a great mystery, perfectly wise and infallibly omniscient, but without consciousness of any kind and therefore without morality. Charles Darwin was to depict it as nothing more than a rapacious power bent on procreation. Intuitively Coleridge sensed that science was heading in this direction. Such a nature would become a paradigm for human thought itself. He held tenaciously to the belief that *the final solution of phaenomenon (Nature) cannot itself be phaenomenon; and next, the law that action and reaction can only take place between things similar in essence* (*The Philosophical Lectures of Samuel Taylor Coleridge*, ed. Kathleen Coburn, Routledge & Kegan Paul, 1949, pp. 145–6) – nature with nature, mind with mind. Nature is always *about to be born*, is always *becoming*, but that which is the originator of its own action must be spiritual or supernatural. This is the side of Coleridge that Wordsworth was unwilling to follow. The separation of mind and nature is a truth Coleridge found not only in post-Kantian idealism but in the Greek philosophers, especially Plato and Pythagoras. If we are to do justice to the *myriad mindedness* of his poetry we need to look at this.

Coleridge believed his mystical poems to be his greatest, work in which he had done justice to the many sides of his genius. He believed that the greatest evil in his age was the polarization of science and nature. It was a pernicious poison injuring the soul and intellect. Experimental science had become agnostic in its methods and materialistic in its principles, pulling philosophy with it. For science, truth is gauged in proportion to the facts accumulated, but religion appeals to the heart; the first appears without proof, but the second without hope. In ancient religions Coleridge saw the *true* balance in *soul* (a word that for us seems to have lost much of its meaning). In *soul* lay the key that would unlock the universe.

What, then, *is* soul for Coleridge? It is a portion of the *Universal Soul*, a speck of the divine spirit, an immortal monad tossed to and fro in an eternal struggle to find happiness. In his life-long preoccupation with ancient religious thought, Coleridge was ceaselessly drawn to the Greek mysteries, especially Prometheus and the cults of Cupid and Psyche; to the Eleusian mysteries, the Egyptian myths of Isis and Osiris, to the esoteric teachings of Indian and Persian religion. These he was able to anchor to Christian mysticism, particularly that of Boehme and Swedenborg, firmly believing that *Christianity is not a Theory, or a Speculation; but a* Life − *not a Philosophy of Life, but a Living Process* (*Aids to Reflection*, ed. J.B. Beer, Princeton University Press, 1993, p. 136). This is what one might call *evolutive and transcendental spiritualism*, where spirit is the only reality and nature is but its changing, ephemeral expression; its dynamics in space and time.

One of Coleridge's most powerful symbols is the fountain (see, for example, his poem *Kubla Khan*). Just as a fountain or a volcano reveals momentarily the secrets of the underworld, so imagination is a fleeting explosion of the divine soul. Human life is only the preparation for this spiritual life and is a series of successive deaths in which the body throws off its imperfections and yields to the pole of attraction − the Sun of Intelligence, or God. Coleridge sees the pre-Christian mystics and Christ as part of one impulse − *in the assertion of original sin the Greek mythology rose and set*. In imagination he hears with Pythagoras at Castalia the song of the nightingales and the music of the fountain.

But Coleridge is not a mystic in the sense of one who puts all else aside and associates fully with supernatural reality by means of love. He is a religious poet in the manner of George Herbert and Gerard Manley Hopkins. Writers such as Boehme help to *keep alive the heart in the head*, supplying him with a mine of rich symbolism − the complex dynamics of the human will, the agonies of creation, the microcosm and the macrocosm, the love of self as the serpent, the closed and expanded senses, the alchemical fire symbol by which things possess a hidden quality which only fire can reveal, the importance of imagination in a system of salvation, a theory of correspondences. It is one of the hazards of poetry that symbolism forces language beyond its intentions. A metaphor or symbol illuminates an object or thought by substituting another, and these changing perspectives are the wonder of the art, but some things can only be expressed through symbol. Coleridge reads the mystics not just for truth and delight but for figures.

Wordsworth is *not* a mystic in the true sense though in the later nineteenth century he was cast in this mould. He toys with pre-existence and the methods of the mystics; he touches on meditation as yielding the tranquillity needed to overcome suffering, but he is interested mainly in this world. There is a strange complex of humility and egoism in him. He admires those who have found humility, who pass unnoticed and are unconscious of their goodness, the pure in heart, heroic yet childlike, the *human* saints. He feels that each individual has a sacredness defined by vulnerability, suffering as well as joy – such as the secret life of the idiot boy who will not say where he has been all night, Edward who refuses to give reasons why he prefers Kilve, the old man travelling who has found *peace so perfect* upon which none should intrude, and Martha Ray, who remains an enigma around whom mystical things happen but who will only say two words. In his exploration of time Wordsworth touches on mysticism in believing that the poet is able to bring to mind absent things as though they are present, but this is no more than an attribute of memory grounded in the experience of ordinary men.

Metaphor and symbol

It is always illuminating to look at the frequency with which certain words are repeated in a poet's work. The following is a list of recurring words in *Lyrical Ballads*: **Wordsworth**: *fair, beauteous, holy/holier, love, blessing, breeze/wind, tears, glee, green, grief, cold,* *rolled, lonely, solitude/solitary, vacancy, humility, tranquillity, eyes/blind/tears, sensations, blood, mystery, humanity, affection, joy, child.* **Coleridge**: *fire, ice, water/springs, jewels, bright, colour, birds, song, serpents, moonlight, starlight, sun/heat, love, loneliness, sadness, eyes, dreams, ghosts, seraphs, angels, demons, prayer, blessing.*

In spite of his fondness for abstract nouns, Wordsworth's words are mostly human sentiments and objects of sense. Coleridge's are religious, visionary and almost apocalyptic.

Look closer at how these metaphors and symbols are used. First, consider the image of the eye. Both poets use it in imaginative ways. Coleridge refers to eyes 19 times in *The Rime of the Ancyent Marinere*! They are *glittering* and *flashing* with associations of hypnosis. He distinguishes between the eyes of sense and the eyes of the spirit, the latter penetrating that *film of familiarity and selfish solicitude*, searching *for visionary views*. Wordsworth uses eyes in a naturalistic way – *all this mighty world/Of eye and ear.* Even his *inward eye* recalls almost photographically past objects and experience. In *Lines left upon a Seat in a Yew-tree* he condemns the man who *Fixing his downward eye, he many an hour/A morbid pleasure nourished...lost man!* (lines 27–28, 40). This is something he criticizes in Coleridge, who always uses eyes to define the expanded senses. For Coleridge, the spiritual eye is connected with dreams, hallucinations, reverie, somnambulism, clairvoyance, a sense seen at work in the oracular powers of Theoclea the Pythoness at Delphi, said to see the vibrations of the rising sun at which she heard celestial songs, and Swedenborg's and Boehme's visions of paradisal light. He believed he had glimpsed this world himself in the experience of *Kubla Khan*. For him, only the spiritual eye can truly see body, soul and spirit and understand good and evil. Evil closes the spiritual eye; good opens it.

Both poets continually refer to moonlight, sunlight and starlight but again in different ways. One of the most stunning images in *The Rime of the Ancyent Marinere* is *The Ocean hath no blast:/His great bright eye most silently/Up to the moon is cast* (lines 420–422). It combines two of Coleridge's favourite images depicting nature's subservience to Christ. In *The Idiot Boy* the moon is equated with lunacy. In *The Thorn*, Martha Ray sits *until the moon/Through half the clear blue sky will go* (lines 203–204), but in both cases moonlight is seen naturalistically. Wordsworth seems drawn to the earth; Coleridge to the heavens. He was fascinated by the moon, in Pythagorean myth said to magnetize the soul for earthly incarnation and demagnetize it for its heavenly abode. He studied the Egyptian symbols of the Sun, the Serpent and the Wings in connection with the divine creation of the world: the sun as eternal generation in the serpent, which is in turn exalted and flies back to the sun.

These images in the story of the Mariner make sense if we realize that Coleridge is possibly alluding to Egyptian temple language in how the killing of a winged creature (the Albatross) destroys the connection between sun (God) and the serpent (Body). The serpent, represented by the water snakes, is the unregenerate flesh which becomes loathsome to the Mariner, while the sun is experienced not as light but heat. Finally, the Mariner is initiated into a sublime mystery, seeing the *true sun*, as Pythagoras, Plato and other mystics have described it. It is not difficult to see a connection between the ancient solar mysteries and Christ as the Light of the World. Thus the moon is reflected light, God's intermediary for man's redemption. There are many winged creatures in Coleridge and he spiritualizes nearly all of them; for Wordsworth, a bird is just a bird.

Both poets deal with extreme forms of imagination and madness. Wordsworth presents madness in its physical sense of disease or senility, but both poets agreed that there is a fine line between genius and madness. Coleridge considered writing a poem on delirium – the Mariner has a touch of it – but physical madness is for him a state in which madness circles within itself whereas genius, or divine madness, is like a fountain of truth. Coleridge talks of *Moon-blasted madness* in *Religious Musings* as a state of fear. His addiction to opium increased his awareness of the unconscious. *Kubla Khan*, published in 1816 as *a psychological curiosity*, is rich with symbols of madness and imagination. In thinking about these aspects of the unconscious in their work, you should bear in mind that Coleridge and Wordsworth lived over a century before Freud.

Activity

Compare the *Rime of the Ancyent Marinere* with one or two poems of Wordsworth's which explore phenomena such as earth, air, fire and water, and light. Explore the different ways in which each poet deals with sense experience.

Discussion

Coleridge's poem is built on the four elements seen through different perspectives, natural and supernatural. In the natural sense these elements can be kindly or cruel – the wind can be benign, joyfully driving the ship, the rain and dew quenches the Mariner's thirst, yet 200 sailors die of exposure to the sun's pitiless fire. In the supernatural sense, the sun's rays and the sea-serpents have mystical implications; there are uncanny flashings and glimmerings. Coleridge may have been thinking of the occult powers of Pythagoras said to have created pantomorphic or astral light, a magic fire which the Egyptians actually called *serpents*. The rising and setting sun is rich with Christian symbolism. The breeze is God's blessing. The angelic beings are creatures of light and sound, close to Plato's codes of colour and music. The mythological associations are endless. Wordsworth's presentation of these things is purely naturalistic. Nature is mostly benign. The female vagrant receives a *heavenly silence* from the sea. Fire brings warmth to Goody Blake. In *Lines, Written at a Small Distance from my House* the poet feels a *blessing in the air* (line 5) and bids his sister *come forth and feel the sun*. The waters of the sylvan Wye bring spiritual peace and he bids the winds *be free/To blow against thee* (lines 137–138). Wordsworth fulfils what he has promised in the Preface: *the Reader will find no personifications of abstract ideas in these volumes* (Appendices, p. 233). For Wordsworth, *here or nowhere is our heaven*.

You do not need to judge which of these two poets has the better perspective, for both are Romantics in the true sense. Study of the poems reveals a fascinating discourse of two minds. As the Mariner's gripping tale finds resonance in the Wedding Guest, and Dorothy serves as the avatar (a living representative or embodiment) of her brother's philosophy of consolation, so the poems continually unfold through successive generations of listeners and interpreters. Both Coleridge and Wordsworth have their disciples who proclaim their poet has the superior vision, yet it is essential for the purpose of understanding the seminal force created by *Lyrical Ballads* to recognize how these two great artists joyfully submerged their differences for the purpose of producing what became a unique collection in the history of English Literature.

The critical background

Of those who read the first edition of *Lyrical Ballads*, most found Wordsworth's language awkward and his subjects in poor taste; a few found them refreshingly true to life. In answer to some unfavourable critics Wordsworth claimed that he had only written it for money. However, the volume became a talking point in literary circles and soon went into a second edition containing Wordsworth's Preface, which helped to establish the work as a contribution to poetic theory. By 1803, Coleridge ceased writing significant poetry and, by 1807, Wordsworth had completed his best work, though he continued to write voluminously – over 450 sonnets alone. In 1843 Wordsworth was appointed Poet Laureate, after which he became an almost saintly figure, particularly for ordinary people, upholding the values of simple piety and arch domesticity. As a mechanized age developed along with industrial squalor, his deification of nature and the English countryside took on the character of lost private and public innocence. After 1850, this laudation increased as the effects of Darwin's theory of natural selection – that nature is based on the survival of the fittest – undermined traditional religious values. In an age of growing doubt there was much consolation to be had from idealizing the lives of country dwellers.

Coleridge's reputation was less assured. The three great poems – *The Rime of the Ancyent Marinere*, *Kubla Khan* and *Christabel* – caught the Victorian Gothic imagination, but Southey reviewed the *Rime of the Ancyent Marinere* with all the bitterness of an old friend. Coleridge's conversation poems, of which *The Nightingale* is an example, influenced all the later Romantic poets, but it was not until 1965 that M.H. Abrams credited Coleridge with originating the true Romantic lyric: an interior monologue in which the poet resolves a mood. Coleridge's lectures on Shakespeare established his reputation as the founder of modern criticism. John Stuart Mill described him as *one of the two great seminal minds of England in their age* [*the other being Bentham*]...*the class of thinkers has scarcely yet arisen, by whom he is to be judged* (*Mill on Bentham and Coleridge*, ed. F.R. Leavis, Chatto & Windus, 1950, p. 40). However, Hazlitt condemned Coleridge's metaphysics as a dead weight which cultivated the image of *the damaged man*. Walter Pater responded sensitively to his German Idealism, though he tried to make it relevant to Victorian sensibility, an effort William Walsh has described as *like looking at a tiger through a lorgnette* (*Coleridge: The Work and the Relevance*, Chatto & Windus, 1967, p. 202). Thomas Carlyle called him spiritually idle and lacking in moral fibre, but Thomas de Quincey paid tribute to his *splendid art of conversation*. By the end of the nineteenth century, Coleridge was primarily interesting to critics as a case in literary genetics and his poetry a species of the abnormal, but his influence on artists has been huge.

Twentieth-century critics began a revaluation of the work of both poets. D.H. Lawrence, who had dismissed Keats and Wordsworth as *post-mortem poets*, admired Coleridge's vitalism, translating his snake imagery into his own thinking. Robert Graves responded enthusiastically, dividing him into *Coleridge entranced and Coleridge un-entranced* ('The integrity of the poet', *The Listener*, 1955, pp. 579–80). T.S. Eliot preferred Wordsworth's good common sense to German sublimity – a reflection of his own struggle with poetic diction in the 1920s – but admitted that *to be a ruined man is itself a vocation* (*The Use of Poetry and the Use of Criticism*, Faber and Faber, 1933, p. 6). A major step to rehabilitate Coleridge's reputation came in the 1930s with the publication of *Road to Xanadu: A Study in the Ways of the Imagination* by John Livingstone Lowes (Constable, 1927). This feat of literary forensic science began the exploration of Coleridge's poems as multi-layered creations arising from his vast reading and having no narrow linear logic but an organic and strange identity of their own. The work exposed Coleridge's unhappiness and addiction.

In the 1930s Kathleen Coburn discovered the *Notebooks*, and it became her life's work to bring them to publication along with the *Letters* and *Marginalia*. She showed that Coleridge was, among other things, a precursor of Freudian psychology. In 1934, Maud Bodkin examined his work in the light of the theories of Carl Jung; I.A. Richards (*Coleridge on Imagination*, Kegan Paul, Trench & Trubner, 1934) promoted his literary criticism. At last it was understood how he had been able to think on many levels simultaneously and how – as Mill had foreseen – his dazzling, though sometimes unstructured, work had been a century ahead of its time.

The most recent criticism is of a specialist kind, ranging from psychoanalysis to marine biology. Among modern poets, Seamus Heaney and Ted Hughes have reflected on his work, the latter seeing two Coleridges – one religious and the other natural (see Hughes, *Winter Pollen: Occasional Prose*, Faber and Faber, 1995). From the many scholars of Coleridge, a few of the most significant are J.B. Beer, who has done justice to Coleridge's life-long mission to retrieve the authority of spiritual texts and myths, and Owen Barfield, whose *What Coleridge Thought* is among the very best work on Coleridge's philosophy and examines his *polar logic*.

Wordsworth has steadily held his place as one of the great Romantics, though he has provoked extreme views. He had a profound influence on Victorian novelists, especially on George

Eliot, the Brontës, Dickens, and Hardy. His concern for the struggles of the poor, a theme that he shared with Dickens, increased his popularity, particularly in Russia. The Victorians read him in the light of the work of Lord Alfred Tennyson (who assumed the Poet Laureate mantle after Wordsworth's death in 1850), focusing on his moral teachings and his concern with childhood innocence. Grasmere became a place of pilgrimage (it still is), although Wordsworth remained an isolated figure, hating any intrusion into his private life, and believing that his poems should speak for themselves. As Wordsworth's early intuitive genius faded, he turned to the Christian faith, even going so far as to Christianize his earlier work and tone down the pagan joy. But having denied the existence of a transcendent or personal God for so long, such faith seemed only half-hearted.

Poets have been equivocal about Wordsworth, though Keats thought him more profound than Milton. Byron and Shelley ridiculed him. Robert Browning believed he had sold the Romantic cause for *a handful of silver*, but he joined the Wordsworth Society when it was formed in 1880. In America, Ralph Waldo Emerson proclaimed that he saw in Wordsworth a precise correspondence between nature, the cognitive mind, language and metaphor. Walt Whitman agreed. Wordsworth's death in 1850 was accompanied by two dramatic events: one was the publication of *The Prelude*, an epic poem describing his life which he had kept concealed for half a century. There are two versions of it, one written in 1805 in the aftermath of the French Revolution, and the other belonging to the late 1840s, to which Wordsworth had added a eulogy to Edmund Burke, the opponent of the revolution. This established Wordsworth's political position as high Tory. The other startling event was the revelation that Wordsworth had an illegitimate daughter in France. Even his sons did not know that they had a half-sister. This information and the later discovery of his passionate love letters to Mary has provided a new perspective on the private and emotional side of Wordsworth's character.

As with Coleridge, the critical heritage has been enormous, and many great scholars have contributed studies of Wordsworth's work: Ernest de Selincourt edited the complete works of Wordsworth between 1940–1954 (Clarendon Press). Helen Darbishire's *The Poet Wordsworth* (Clarendon Press, 1950) reinvigorated his reputation. F.W. Bateson's *Wordsworth: A Re-interpretation* (Longman, 1963) helped to balance some spiteful carping by F.R. Leavis and William Empson. Mary Moorman produced a definitive biography in 1968 (two volumes, Clarendon Press). More recent biographies include those by Hunter Davis (Weidenfeld & Nicolson, 1980) and Stephen Gill (Oxford University Press, 1990). Juliet Barker's *Wordsworth: A Life* (Viking, 2000), though massively detailed, is biased against Coleridge. John Beer's *Wordsworth and the Human Heart* (Macmillan, 1978) is, in my opinion, like all his criticism, sensitive and balanced. The standard edition of Wordsworth's poetry edited by Stephen Parrish (Cornell University Press, 1975) is still an authoritative text.

Coleridge remains startlingly modern. His belief that we cannot believe anything of God but what we find in ourselves has a particular resonance for our own times and does not contradict his Christian faith. His reputation has been controversial because he rejected all systems and dogmas. Wordsworth, with his stoicism, good sense and moral certainty that man is essentially good if left alone, may seem too simplistic in a rootless and media-driven society such as ours, but his greatness and originality as one of the two Romantic revolutionaries is unquestioned and the continuing partisan interpretation of his work looks increasingly absurd. The Victorians took heart from his words in *Afterthought* to *Sonnets on The River Duddon*

> ...as toward the silent tomb we go,
> Through love, through hope, and faith's transcendent dower,
> We feel that we are greater than we know.

Such sentiments do not translate easily into our world, but if we do not have an alternative philosophy of hope, we would be rather foolish to scorn them.

Essay Questions

These questions are designed to test your textual insight, your thoughts on language and structure and your knowledge of period and genre. Some may be adapted to include one other comparative text not found in *Lyrical Ballads* but located within the Romantic tradition. The questions may be used to consolidate your work for synoptic papers.

1 *Searching for more and more heightened states of feeling is dangerous to poetry.* How far does this statement apply to these poems and to other nineteenth-century Romantic poems which you have read?

2 Do you think the intention of creating a single work has been achieved? Consider how far the poems express the different characters and views of their authors.

3 Many of these poems deal with the changing moods of nature. Choose and examine **two** or **three** poems that illustrate these effects on human life.

4 Is *The Rime of the Ancyent Marinere* the greatest poem in *Lyrical Ballads*? Compare it with **one** other in the Romantic tradition that you believe to be of equal importance.

5 *Literalness is responsible for his profundity and narrowness alike, his obstinacy, his very limited powers of self-criticism, his feeble sense of humour, his plain dullness* (J. Jones, *The Egotistical Sublime*, Chatto & Windus, 1964, p. 16). Is this too harsh a judgement of Wordsworth's work in this collection?

6 Why do you think this volume was so influential to later writers and how truly revolutionary was it? Your answer should include some reference to the Preface.

7 Discuss the main religious and moral values enshrined in *Lyrical Ballads*.

8 What do these poems reveal about the state of the poor in England in 1798? Make close reference to at least **two** or **three** poems in your essay.

9 Thanks to the human heart by which we live,
Thanks to its tenderness, its joys, and fears,
To me the meanest flower that blows can give
Thoughts that do often lie too deep for tears.

What light do these closing lines of Wordsworth's *Ode on the Intimations of Immortality* throw upon his achievement in *Lyrical Ballads*?

10 *Romanticism is blighted by a sense of loss; loss of innocence, loss of Paradise, loss of love.* Do you agree? What historical and cultural conditions might have produced this mood?

11 Explore **two** or **three** poems that demonstrate an experience of the sublime.

12 Explore what the two poets have to say about disturbed mental states, showing how individuals deal with a breakdown of stability in their personal lives. Make close reference to at least **two** or **three** poems in your essay.

13 Writing in 1876, George Eliot described her novels as *a set of experiments in life to keep hold of something more sure than shifting theory.* Would this be a fair description of the experiments in *Lyrical Ballads* and do they succeed?

Chronology

The time-chart below offers an outline of events in the life of Wordsworth and Coleridge, listed against what was happening in British and European history, to help you put their lives into an appropriate context and give you background to the changing focus of their writing.

Year	Artistic context	Historical context
1751	Gray's *Elegy written in a Country Churchyard*	
1769–1790	Sir Joshua Reynold's *Discourses on the Rules of Art* (lectures to students at the Royal Academy)	
1770	Wordsworth born on 7 April at Cockermouth, Cumberland, son of John, land agent to Sir James Lowther, and Ann Cookson	
1772	Coleridge born on 21 October at Ottery St Mary, Devon	
1774		Arkwright's first spinning mill Watt's steam engine American Revolution.
1775–1783		
1779–1781	Dr Johnson's *Lives of the Poets* Wordsworth sent to Hawkshead Grammar School (until 1787)	
1782	Coleridge sent to Christ's Hospital School, London	
1783	Wordsworth's father dies. Family broken up.	Declaration of American Independence
1788	Wordsworth goes to St John's College, Cambridge Birth of Lord Byron	

Year	Artistic context	Historical context
1789	Blake's *Songs of Innocence*	14 July: Fall of the Bastille
1790	Wordsworth on walking tour of the Alps	
1791	September: Coleridge goes up to Jesus College, Cambridge	Reign of Terror in France
	Burke's *Reflections on the Revolution*	
	Thomas Paine's *Rights of Man*	
1792	Mary Wollstonecraft's *Vindications of the Rights of Woman*	
	Wordsworth in France. Falls in love with Annette Vallon (1766–1841). Their daughter Caroline born, Dec. 1792	September Massacres
1793	William Godwin's *Inquiry into Political Justice*	Execution of Louis XVI
		England at war with France
1794	Wordsworth receives a legacy of £900 from Raisley Calvert	
1795	Birth of John Keats	
	August: Wordsworth and Coleridge meet in Bristol	
	September: Wordsworth and his sister at Racedown Lodge	
	October: Coleridge marries Sara Fricker	
1796	Coleridge on speaking tour in the Midlands and the north of England	
	April: Coleridge's *Poems on Various Subjects* published	
	September: Hartley Coleridge born	
	December: Coleridge and his wife move to Nether Stowey, Somerset	

Year	Artistic context	Historical context
1797	July: The Wordsworths move to Alfoxden House. Plans begin for an edition of *Lyrical Ballads* October: Coleridge writes *Kubla Khan* at Ash Farm, Culborne November: *The Rime of the Ancyent Marinere* planned	
1798	First edition of *Lyrical Ballads* published	
1799	Summer: Wordsworth and Coleridge return from a tour of Germany October: Coleridge makes his first tour of the Lake District	Napoleon becomes First Consul
1800	Coleridge moves to Greta Hall, Keswick in the Lake District Second edition of *Lyrical Ballads* published with first Preface	
1802	October: Wordsworth marries Mary Hutchinson	
1803	Coleridge becomes Secretary to the Governor of Malta	First General Enclosure Act
1805	Wordsworth's brother John drowns	Battle of Trafalgar
1810	Wordsworth and Coleridge quarrel	
1812	Wordsworth and Coleridge are reconciled	
1834	Death of Coleridge	
1843	Wordsworth appointed Poet Laureate	
1850	Death of Wordsworth	

Appendices

Wordsworth's Preface of 1800

The first Volume of these Poems has already been submitted to general perusal. It was published, as an experiment which, I hoped, might be of some use to ascertain, how far, by fitting to metrical arrangement a selection of the real language of men in a state of vivid sensation, that sort of pleasure and that quantity of pleasure may be imparted, which a Poet may rationally endeavour to impart.

I had formed no very inaccurate estimate of the probable effect of those Poems: I flattered myself that they who should be pleased with them would read them with more than common pleasure: and on the other hand I was well aware that by those who should dislike them they would be read with more than common dislike. The result has differed from my expectation in this only, that I have pleased a greater number, than I ventured to hope I should please.

For the sake of variety and from a consciousness of my own weakness I was induced to request the assistance of a Friend, who furnished me with the Poems of the Ancient Mariner, the Foster-Mother's Tale, the Nightingale, the Dungeon, and the Poem entitled Love. I should not, however, have requested this assistance, had I not believed that the poems of my Friend would in a great measure have the same tendency as my own, and that, though there would be found a difference, there would be found no discordance in the colours of our style; as our opinions on the subject of poetry do almost entirely coincide.

Several of my Friends are anxious for the success of these Poems from a belief, that if the views, with which they were composed, were indeed realized, a class of Poetry would be produced, well adapted to interest mankind permanently, and not unimportant in the multiplicity and in the quality of its moral relations: and on this account they have advised me to prefix a systematic defence of the theory, upon which the poems were written. But I was unwilling to undertake the task, because I knew that on this occasion the Reader would look coldly upon my arguments, since I might be suspected of having been principally influenced by the selfish and foolish hope of *reasoning* him into an approbation of these particular Poems: and I was still more unwilling to undertake the task, because adequately to display my opinions and fully to enforce my arguments would require a space wholly disproportionate to the nature of a preface. For to treat the subject with the clearness and coherence, of which I believe it susceptible, it would be necessary to give a full account of the present state of the public taste in this country, and to determine how far this taste is healthy or depraved; which again could not be determined, without pointing out, in what manner language and the human mind act and react on each other, and without retracing the revolutions not of literature alone but likewise of society itself. I have therefore altogether declined to enter regularly upon this defence; yet I am sensible, that there would be some impropriety in abruptly obtruding upon the Public, without a few words of introduction, Poems so materially different from those, upon which general approbation is at present bestowed.

It is supposed, that by the act of writing in verse an Author makes a formal engagement that he will gratify certain known habits of association, that he not only thus apprizes the Reader that certain classes of ideas and expressions will be found in his book, but that others will be carefully excluded. This exponent or symbol held forth by metrical language must in different æras of literature have excited very different expectations: for example, in the age of Catullus Terence and Lucretia, and that of Statius or Claudian, and in our own country, in the age of Shakespeare and Beaumont and Fletcher, and that of Donne and Cowley, or Dryden, or Pope. I will not take upon me to determine the exact import of the promise which by the act of writing in verse an Author in the present day makes to his Reader; but I am certain it will appear to many persons that I have not fulfilled the terms of an engagement thus voluntarily contracted. I hope therefore the Reader will not censure me, if I attempt to state what I have proposed to myself to perform, and also, (as far as the limits of a preface will permit) to explain some of the chief reasons which have determined me in the choice of my purpose: that at least he may be spared any unpleasant feeling of disappointment, and that I myself may be protected from the most dishonorable accusation which can be brought against an Author, namely, that of an indolence which prevents him from endeavouring to ascertain what is his duty, or, when his duty is ascertained prevents him from performing it.

The principal object then which I proposed to myself in these Poems was to make the incidents of common life interesting by tracing in them, truly though not ostentatiously, the primary laws of our nature: chiefly as far as regards the manner in which we associate ideas in a state of excitement. Low and rustic life was generally chosen because in that situation the essential passions of the heart find a better soil in which they can attain their maturity, are less under restraint, and speak a plainer and more emphatic language; because in that situation our elementary feelings exist in a state of greater simplicity and consequently may be more accurately contemplated and more forcibly communicated; because the manners of rural life germinate from those elementary feelings; and from the necessary character of rural occupations are more easily comprehended; and are more durable; and lastly, because in that situation the passions of men are incorporated with the beautiful and permanent forms of nature. The language too of these men is adopted (purified indeed from what appear to be its real defects, from all lasting and rational causes of dislike or disgust) because such men hourly communicate with the best objects from which the best part of language is originally derived; and because, from their rank in society and the sameness and narrow circle of their intercourse, being less under the action of social vanity they convey their feelings and notions in simple and unelaborated expressions. Accordingly such a language arising out of repeated experience and regular feelings is a more permanent and a far more philosophical language than that which is frequently substituted for it by Poets, who think that they are conferring honour upon themselves and their art in proportion as they separate themselves from the sympathies of men, and indulge in arbitrary and capricious habits of expression in order to furnish food for fickle tastes and fickle appetites of their own creation.*

I cannot be insensible of the present outcry against the triviality and meanness both of thought and language, which some of my contemporaries have occasionally introduced into their metrical compositions, and I acknowledge that this defect where it exists, is more dishonorable to the Writer's own character than false refinement or arbitrary innovation, though I should contend at the same time that it is far less pernicious in the sum of its consequences. From such verses the Poems in these volumes will be found distinguished at least by one mark of difference, that each of them has a worthy *purpose*. Not that I mean to say, that I always began to write with a distinct purpose formally conceived; but I believe that my habits of meditation have so formed my feelings, as that my descriptions of such objects as strongly excite those feelings, will be found to carry along with them a *purpose*. If in this opinion I am mistaken I can have little right to the name of a Poet. For all good poetry is the spontaneous overflow of powerful feelings; but though this be true, Poems to which any value can be attached, were never produced on any variety of subjects but by a man who being possessed of more than usual organic sensibility had also thought long and deeply. For our continued influxes of feeling are modified and directed by our thoughts, which are indeed the representatives of all our past feelings; and as by contemplating the relation of these general representatives to each other, we discover what is really important to men, so by the repetition and continuance of this act feelings connected with important subjects will be nourished, till at length,

---

* It is worth while here to observe that the affecting parts of Chaucer are almost always expressed in language pure and universally intelligible even to this day.

if we be originally possessed of much organic sensibility, such habits of mind will be produced that by obeying blindly and mechanically the impulses of those habits we shall describe objects and utter sentiments of such a nature and in such connection with each other, that the understanding of the being to whom we address ourselves, if he be in a healthful state of association, must necessarily be in some degree enlightened, his taste exalted, and his affections ameliorated.

I have said that each of these poems has a purpose. I have also informed my Reader what this purpose will be found principally to be: namely to illustrate the manner in which our feelings and ideas are associated in a state of excitement. But speaking in less general language, it is to follow the fluxes and refluxes of the mind when agitated by the great and simple affections of our nature. This object I have endeavoured in these short essays to attain by various means; by tracing the maternal passion through many of its more subtle windings, as in the poems of the IDIOT BOY and the MAD MOTHER; by accompanying the last struggles of a human being at the approach of death, cleaving in solitude to life and society, as in the Poem of the FORSAKEN INDIAN; by shewing, as in the Stanzas entitled WE ARE SEVEN, the perplexity and obscurity which in childhood attend our notion of death, or rather our utter inability to admit that notion; or by displaying the strength of fraternal, or to speak more philosophically, of moral attachment when early associated with the great and beautiful objects of nature, as in THE BROTHERS; or, as in the Incident of SIMON LEE, by placing my Reader in the way of receiving from ordinary moral sensations another and more salutary impression than we are accustomed to receive from them. It has also been part of my general purpose to attempt to sketch characters under the influence of less impassioned feelings, as in the OLD MAN TRAVELLING, THE TWO THIEVES, &c. characters of which the elements are simple, belonging rather to nature than to manners, such as exist now and will probably always exist, and which from their constitution may be distinctly and profitably contemplated. I will not abuse the indulgence of my Reader by dwelling longer upon this subject; but it is proper that I should mention one other circumstance which distinguishes these Poems from the popular Poetry of the day; it is this, that the feeling therein developed gives importance to the action and situation and not the action and situation to the feeling. My meaning will be rendered perfectly intelligible by referring my Reader to the Poems entitled POOR SUSAN and the CHILDLESS FATHER, particularly to the last Stanza of the latter Poem.

I will not suffer a sense of false modesty to prevent me from asserting, that I point my Reader's attention to this mark of distinction far less for the sake of these particular Poems than from the general importance of the subject. The subject is indeed important! For the human mind is capable of excitement without the application of gross and violent stimulants; and he must have a very faint perception of its beauty and dignity who does not know this, and who does not further know that one being is elevated above another in proportion as he possesses this capability. It has therefore appeared to me that to endeavour to produce or enlarge this capability is one of the best services in which, at any period, a Writer can be engaged; but this service, excellent at all times, is especially so at the present day. For a multitude of causes unknown to former times are now acting with a combined force to blunt the discriminating powers of the mind, and unfitting it for all voluntary exertion to reduce it to a state of almost savage torpor. The most effective of these causes are the great national events which are daily taking place, and the increasing accumulation of men in cities, where the uniformity of their occupations produces a craving for extraordinary incident which the rapid communication of intelligence hourly gratifies. To this tendency of life and manners the literature and theatrical exhibitions of the country have conformed themselves. The invaluable works of our elder writers, I had almost said the works of Shakespear and Milton, are driven into neglect by frantic novels, sickly and stupid German Tragedies, and deluges of idle and extravagant stories in verse. – When I think upon this degrading thirst after outrageous stimulation I am almost ashamed to have spoken of the feeble effort with which I have endeavoured to counteract it; and reflecting upon the magnitude of the general evil, I should be oppressed with no dishonorable melancholy, had I not a deep impression of certain inherent and indestructible qualities of the human mind, and likewise of certain powers in the great and permanent objects that act upon it which are equally inherent and indestructible; and did I not further add to this impression a belief that the time is approaching when the evil will be systematically opposed by men of greater powers and with far more distinguished success.

Having dwelt thus long on the subjects and aim of these Poems, I shall request the Reader's permission to apprize him of a few circumstances relating to their *style*, in order, among other reasons, that I may not be censured for not having performed what I never attempted. Except in a very few instances the Reader will find no personifications of abstract ideas in these volumes, not that I mean to censure such personifications: they may be well fitted for certain sorts of composition, but in these Poems I propose to myself to imitate, and, as far as possible, to adopt the very language of men, and I do not find that such personifications make any regular or natural part of that language. I wish to keep my Reader in the company of flesh and blood, persuaded that by so doing I shall interest him. Not but that I believe that others who pursue a different track may interest him likewise: I do not interfere with their claim, I only wish to prefer a different claim of my own. There will also be found in these volumes little of what is usually called poetic diction; I have taken as much pains to avoid it as others ordinarily take to produce it; this I have done for the reason already alleged, to bring my language near to the language of men, and further, because the pleasure which I have proposed to myself to impart is of a kind very different from that which is supposed by many persons to be the proper object of poetry. I do not know how without being culpably particular I can give my Reader a more exact notion of the style in which I wished these poems to be written than by informing him that I have at all times endeavoured to look steadily at my subject, consequently I hope it will be found that there is in these Poems little falsehood of description, and that my ideas are expressed in language fitted to their respective importance. Something I must have gained by this practice, as it is friendly to one property of all good poetry, namely good sense; but it has necessarily cut me off from a large portion of phrases and figures of speech which from father to son have long been regarded as the common inheritance of Poets. I have also thought it expedient to restrict myself still further, having abstained from the use of many expressions, in themselves proper and beautiful, but which have been foolishly repeated by bad Poets till such feelings of disgust are connected with them as it is scarcely possible by any art of association to overpower.

If in a Poem there should be found a series of lines, or even a single line, in which the language, though naturally arranged and according to the strict laws of metre, does not differ from that of prose, there is a numerous class of critics who, when they stumble upon these prosaisms as they call them, imagine that they have made a notable discovery, and exult over the Poet as over a man ignorant of his own profession. Now these men would establish a canon of criticism which the Reader will conclude he must utterly reject if he wishes to be pleased with these volumes. And it would be a most easy task to prove to him that not only the language of a large portion of every good poem, even of the most elevated character, must necessarily, except with reference to the metre, in no respect differ from that of good prose, but likewise that some of the most interesting parts of the best poems will be found to be strictly the language of prose when prose is well written. The truth of this assertion might be demonstrated by innumerable passages from almost all the poetical writings, even of Milton himself. I have not space for much quotation; but, to illustrate the subject in a general manner, I will here adduce a short composition of Gray, who was at the head of those who by their reasonings have attempted to widen the space of separation betwixt Prose and Metrical composition, and was more than any other man curiously elaborate in the structure of his own poetic diction.

> In vain to me the smiling mornings shine,
> And reddening Phœbus lifts his golden fire:
> The birds in vain their amorous descant join,
> Or chearful fields resume their green attire:
> These ears alas! for other notes repine;
> *A different object do these eyes require;*
> *My lonely anguish melts no heart but mine;*
> *And in my breast the imperfect joys expire;*
> Yet Morning smiles the busy race to cheer,
> And new-born pleasure brings to happier men;
> The fields to all their wonted tribute bear;
> To warm their little loves the birds complain.
> *I fruitless mourn to him that cannot hear*
> *And weep the more because I weep in vain.*

It will easily be perceived that the only part of this Sonnet which is of any value is the lines printed in Italics: it is equally obvious that except in the rhyme, and in the use of the single word 'fruitless' for fruitlessly, which is so far a defect, the language of these lines does in no respect differ from that of prose.

Is there then, it will be asked, no essential difference between the language of prose and metrical composition? I answer that there neither is nor can be any essential difference. We are fond of tracing the resemblance between Poetry and Painting, and, accordingly, we call them Sisters: but where shall we find bonds of connection sufficiently strict to typify the affinity betwixt metrical and prose composition? They both speak by and to the same organs; the bodies in which both of them are clothed may be said to be of the same substance, their affections are kindred and almost identical, not necessarily differing even in degree;* Poetry sheds no tears 'such as Angels weep,' but natural and

---

* I here use the word 'Poetry' (though against my own judgment) as opposed to the word Prose, and synonomous with metrical composition. But much confusion has been introduced into criticism by this contradistinction of Poetry and Prose, instead of the more philosophical one of Poetry and Science. The only strict antithesis to Prose is Metre.

human tears; she can boast of no celestial Ichor that distinguishes her vital juices from those of prose; the same human blood circulates through the veins of them both.

If it be affirmed that rhyme and metrical arrangement of themselves constitute a distinction which overturns what I have been saying on the strict affinity of metrical language with that of prose, and paves the way for other distinctions which the mind voluntarily admits, I answer that [see the Note on page 244 for Wordsworth's addition to the text here for the 1802 Preface] the distinction of rhyme and metre is regular and uniform, and not, like that which is produced by what is usually called poetic diction, arbitrary and subject to infinite caprices upon which no calculation whatever can be made. In the one case the Reader is utterly at the mercy of the Poet respecting what imagery or diction he may choose to connect with the passion, whereas in the other the metre obeys certain laws, to which the Poet and Reader both willingly submit because they are certain, and because no interference is made by them with the passion but such as the concurring testimony of ages has shewn to heighten and improve the pleasure which coexists with it.

It will now be proper to answer an obvious question, namely, why, professing these opinions have I written in verse? To this in the first place I reply, because, however I may have restricted myself, there is still left open to me what confessedly constitutes the most valuable object of all writing whether in prose or verse, the great and universal passions of men, the most general and interesting of their occupations, and the entire world of nature, from which I am at liberty to supply myself with endless combinations of forms and imagery. Now, granting for a moment that whatever is interesting in these objects may be as vividly described in prose, why am I to be condemned if to such description I have endeavoured to superadd the charm which by the consent of all nations is acknowledged to exist in metrical language? To this it will be answered, that a very small part of the pleasure given by Poetry depends upon the metre, and that it is injudicious to write in metre unless it be accompanied with the other artificial distinctions of style with which metre is usually accompanied, and that by such deviation more will be lost from the shock which will be thereby given to the Reader's associations than will be counterbalanced by any pleasure which he can derive from the general power of numbers. In answer to those who thus contend for the necessity of accompanying metre with certain appropriate colours of style in order to the accomplishment of its appropriate end, and who also, in my opinion, greatly under-rate the power of metre in itself, it might perhaps be almost sufficient to observe that poems are extant, written upon more humble subjects, and in a more naked and simple style than what I have aimed at, which poems have continued to give pleasure from generation to generation. Now, if nakedness and simplicity be a defect, the fact here mentioned affords a strong presumption that poems somewhat less naked and simple are capable of affording pleasure at the present day; and all that I am now attempting is to justify myself for having written under the impression of this belief.

But I might point out various causes why, when the style is manly, and the subject of some importance, words metrically arranged will long continue to impart such a pleasure to mankind as he who is sensible of the extent of that pleasure will be desirous to impart. The end of Poetry is to produce excitement in coexistence with an overbalance of pleasure. Now, by the supposition, excitement is an unusual and irregular state of the mind; ideas and feelings do not in that state succeed each other in accustomed order. But if the words by which this excitement is produced are in themselves powerful, or the images and feelings have an undue proportion of pain connected with them, there is some danger that the excitement may be carried beyond its proper bounds. Now the co-presence of something regular, something to which the mind has been accustomed when in an unexcited or a less excited state, cannot but have great efficacy in tempering and restraining the passion by an intertexture of ordinary feeling. This may be illustrated by appealing to the Reader's own experience of the reluctance with which he comes to the re-perusal of the distressful parts of Clarissa Harlowe, or the Gamester. While Shakespeare's writings, in the most pathetic scenes, never act upon us as pathetic beyond the bounds of pleasure – an effect which is in a great degree to be ascribed to small, but continual and regular impulses of pleasurable surprise from the metrical arrangement. – On the other hand (what it must be allowed will much more frequently happen) if the Poet's words should be incommensurate with the passion, and inadequate to raise the Reader to a height of desirable excitement, then, (unless the Poet's choice of his metre has been grossly injudicious) in the feelings of pleasure which the Reader has been accustomed to connect with metre in general, and in the feeling, whether chearful or melancholy, which he has been accustomed to connect with that particular movement of metre, there will be found something which will greatly contribute to impart passion to the words, and to effect the complex end which the Poet proposes to himself.

If I had undertaken a systematic defence of the theory upon which these poems are written, it would have been my duty to develope the various causes upon which the pleasure received from metrical language depends. Among the chief of these causes is to be reckoned a principle which must be well known to those who have made any of the Arts the object of accurate reflection; I mean the pleasure which the mind derives from the perception of similitude in dissimilitude. This principle is the great spring of the activity of our minds and their chief feeder. From this principle the direction of the sexual appetite, and all the passions connected with it take their origin: It is the life of our ordinary conversation; and upon the accuracy with which similitude in dissimilitude, and dissimilitude in similitude are perceived, depend our taste and our moral feelings. It would not have been a useless employment to have applied this principle to the consideration of metre, and to have shewn that metre is hence enabled to afford much pleasure, and to have pointed out in what manner that pleasure is produced. But my limits will not permit me to enter upon this subject, and I must content myself with a general summary.

I have said that Poetry is the spontaneous overflow of powerful feelings: it takes its origin from emotion recollected in tranquillity: the emotion is contemplated till by a species of reaction the tranquillity gradually disappears, and an emotion, similar to that which was before the subject of contemplation, is gradually produced, and does itself actually exist in the mind. In this mood successful composition generally begins, and in a mood similar to this it is carried on; but the emotion, of whatever kind and in whatever degree, from various causes is qualified by various pleasures, so that in describing any passions whatsoever, which are voluntarily described, the mind will upon the whole be in a state of enjoyment. Now if Nature be thus cautious in preserving in a state of enjoyment a being thus employed, the Poet ought to profit by the lesson thus held forth to him, and ought especially to take care, that whatever passions he communicates to his Reader, those passions, if his Reader's mind be sound and vigorous, should always be accompanied with an overbalance of pleasure. Now the music of harmonious metrical language, the sense of difficulty overcome, and the blind association of pleasure which has been previously received from works of rhyme or metre of the same or similar construction, all these imperceptibly make up a complex feeling of delight, which is of the most important use in tempering the painful feeling which will always be found intermingled with powerful descriptions of the deeper passions. This effect is always produced in pathetic and impassioned poetry; while in lighter compositions the ease and gracefulness with which the Poet manages his numbers are themselves confessedly a principal source of the gratification of the Reader. I might perhaps include all which it is *necessary* to say upon this subject by affirming what few persons will deny, that of two descriptions either of passions, manners, or characters, each of them equally well executed, the one in prose and the other in verse, the verse will be read a hundred times where the prose is read once. We see that Pope by the power of verse alone, has contrived to render the plainest common sense interesting, and even frequently to invest it with the appearance of passion. In consequence of these convictions I related in metre the Tale of GOODY BLAKE and HARRY GILL, which is one of the rudest of this collection. I wished to draw attention to the truth that the power of the human imagination is sufficient to produce such changes even in our physical nature as might almost appear miraculous. The truth is an important one; the fact (for it is a *fact*) is a valuable illustration of it. And I have the satisfaction of knowing that it has been communicated to many hundreds of people who would never have heard of it, had it not been narrated as a Ballad, and in a more impressive metre than is usual in Ballads.

Having thus adverted to a few of the reasons why I have written in verse, and why I have chosen subjects from common life, and endeavoured to bring my language near to the real language of men, if I have been too minute in pleading my own cause, I have at the same time been treating a subject of general interest; and it is for this reason that I request the Reader's permission to add a few words with reference solely to these particular poems, and to some defects which will probably be found in them. I am sensible that my associations must have sometimes been particular instead of general, and that, consequently, giving to things a false importance, sometimes from diseased impulses I may have written upon unworthy subjects; but I am less apprehensive on this account, than that my language may frequently have suffered from those arbitrary connections of feelings and ideas with particular words, from which no man can altogether protect himself. Hence I have no doubt that in some instances feelings even of the ludicrous may be given to my Readers by expressions which appeared to me tender and pathetic. Such faulty expressions, were I convinced they were faulty at present, and that they must necessarily continue to be so, I would willingly take all reasonable pains to correct. But it is dangerous to make these alterations on the simple authority of a few individuals, or even of certain classes of men; for where the understanding of an Author is not convinced, or his feelings altered, this cannot be done without great injury to himself: for his own feelings are his stay and support, and if he sets them aside in one instance, he may be induced to repeat this act till his mind loses all confidence in itself and becomes utterly debilitated. To this it may be added, that the Reader ought never to forget that he is himself exposed to the same errors as the Poet, and perhaps in a much greater degree: for there can be no presumption in saying that it is not probable he will be so well acquainted with the various stages of meaning through which words have passed, or with the fickleness or stability of the relations of particular ideas to each other; and above all, since he is so much less interested in the subject, he may decide lightly and carelessly.

Long as I have detained my Reader, I hope he will permit me to caution him against a mode of false criticism which has been applied to Poetry in which the language closely resembles that of life and nature. Such verses have been triumphed over in parodies of which Dr. Johnson's Stanza is a fair specimen.

'I put my hat upon my head,
And walk'd into the Strand,
And there I met another man
Whose hat was in his hand.'

Immediately under these lines I will place one of the most justly admired stanzas of the '*Babes* in the Wood.'

'These pretty Babes with hand in hand
Went wandering up and down;
But never more they saw the Man
Approaching from the Town.'

In both of these stanzas the words, and the order of the words, in no respect differ from the most unimpassioned conversation. There are words in both, for example, 'the Strand,' and 'the Town,' connected with none but the most familiar ideas; yet the one stanza we admit as admirable, and the other as a fair example of the superlatively contemptible. Whence arises this difference? Not from the metre, not from the language, not from the order of the words; but the *matter* expressed in Dr. Johnson's stanza is contemptible. The proper method of treating trivial and simple verses to which Dr. Johnson's stanza would be a fair parallelism is not to say this is a bad kind of poetry, or this is not poetry, but this wants sense; it is neither interesting in itself, nor can *lead* to any thing interesting; the images neither originate in that sane state of feeling which arises out of thought, nor can excite thought or feeling in the Reader. This is the only sensible manner of dealing with such verses: Why trouble yourself about the species till you have previously decided upon the genus? Why take pains to prove that an Ape is not a Newton when it is self-evident that he is not a man.

I have one request to make of my Reader, which is, that in judging these Poems he would decide by his own feelings genuinely, and not by reflection upon what will probably be the judgment of others. How common is it to hear a person say, 'I myself do not object to this style of composition or this or that expression, but to such and such classes of people it will appear mean or ludicrous.' This mode of criticism so destructive of all sound unadulterated judgment is almost universal: I have therefore to request that the Reader would abide independently by his own feelings, and that if he finds himself affected he would not suffer such conjectures to interfere with his pleasure.

If an Author by any single composition has impressed us with respect for his talents, it is useful to consider this as affording a presumption, that, on other occasions where we have been displeased, he nevertheless may not have written ill or absurdly; and, further, to give him so much credit for this one composition as may induce us to review what has displeased us with more care than we should otherwise have bestowed upon it. This is not only an act of justice, but in our decisions upon poetry especially, may conduce in a high degree to the improvement of our own taste: for an *accurate* taste in Poetry and in all the other arts, as Sir Joshua Reynolds has observed, is an *acquired* talent, which can only be produced by thought and a long continued intercourse with the best models of composition. This is mentioned not with so ridiculous a purpose as to prevent the most inexperienced Reader from judging for himself, (I have already said that I wish him to judge for himself;) but merely to temper the rashness of decision, and to suggest that if Poetry be a subject on which much time has not been bestowed, the judgment may be erroneous, and that in many cases it necessarily will be so.

I know that nothing would have so effectually contributed to further the end which I have in view as to have shewn of what kind the pleasure is, and how the pleasure is produced which is confessedly produced by metrical composition essentially different from what I have here endeavoured to recommend; for the Reader will say that he has been pleased by such composition and what can I do more for him? The power of any art is limited and he will suspect that if I propose to furnish him with new friends it is only upon condition of his abandoning his old friends. Besides, as I have said, the Reader is himself conscious of the pleasure which he has received from such composition, composition to which he has peculiarly attached the endearing name of Poetry; and all men feel an habitual gratitude, and something of an honorable bigotry for the objects which have long continued to please them: we not only wish to be pleased, but to be pleased in that particular way in which we have been accustomed to be pleased. There is a host of arguments in these feelings; and I should be the less able to combat them successfully, as I am willing to allow, that, in order entirely to enjoy the Poetry which I am recommending, it would be necessary to give up much of what is ordinarily enjoyed. But would my limits have permitted me to point out how this pleasure is produced, I might have removed many obstacles, and assisted my Reader in perceiving that the powers of language are not so limited as he may suppose; and that it is possible that poetry may give other enjoyments, of a purer, more lasting, and more exquisite nature. But this part of my subject I have been obliged altogether to omit: as it has been less my present aim to prove that the interest excited by some other kinds of poetry is less vivid, and less worthy of the nobler powers of the mind, than to offer reasons for presuming, that, if the object which I have proposed to myself were adequately attained, a species of poetry would be produced, which is genuine poetry; in its nature well adapted to interest mankind permanently, and likewise important in the multiplicity and quality of its moral relations.

From what has been said, and from a perusal of the Poems, the Reader will be able clearly to perceive the object which I have proposed to myself: he will determine how far I have attained this object; and, what is a much more important question, whether it be worth attaining; and upon the decision of these two questions will rest my claim to the approbation of the public.

Note from Wordsworth's Preface of 1802

In the 1802 edition, Wordsworth changed the rest of this sentence by adding the following text (over 240 lines), after 'I answer that' on page 236:

I answer that the language of such Poetry as I am recommending is, as far as is possible, a selection of the language really spoken by men; that this selection, wherever it is made with true taste and feeling, will of itself form a distinction far greater than would at first be imagined, and will entirely separate the composition from the vulgarity and meanness of ordinary life; and, if metre be superadded thereto, I believe that a dissimilitude will be produced altogether sufficient for the gratification of a rational mind. What other distinction would we have? Whence is it to come? And where is it to exist? Not, surely, where the Poet speaks through the mouths of his characters: it cannot be necessary here, either for elevation of style, or any of its supposed ornaments: for, if the Poet's subject be judiciously chosen, it will naturally, and upon fit occasion, lead him to passions the language of which, if selected truly and judiciously, must necessarily be dignified and variegated, and alive with metaphors and figures. I forbear to speak of an incongruity which would shock the intelligent Reader, should the Poet interweave any foreign splendour of his own with that which the passion naturally suggests: it is sufficient to say that such addition is unnecessary. And, surely, it is more probable that those passages, which with propriety abound with metaphors and figures, will have their due effect, if, upon other occasions where the passions are of a milder character, the style also be subdued and temperate.

But, as the pleasure which I hope to give by the Poems I now present to the Reader must depend entirely on just notions upon this subject, and, as it is in itself of the highest importance to our taste and moral feelings, I cannot content myself with these detached remarks. And if, in what I am about to say, it shall appear to some that my labour is unnecessary, and that I am like a man fighting a battle without enemies, I would remind such persons, that, whatever may be the language outwardly holden by men, a practical faith in the opinions which I am wishing to establish is almost unknown. If my conclusions are admitted, and carried as far as they must be carried if admitted at all, our judgments concerning the works of the greatest Poets both ancient and modern will be far different from what they are at present, both when we praise, and when we censure: and our moral feelings influencing, and influenced by these judgments will, I believe, be corrected and purified.

Taking up the subject, then, upon general grounds, I ask what is meant by the word Poet? What is a Poet? To whom does he address himself? And what language is to be expected from him? He is a man speaking to men: a man, it is true, endued with more lively sensibility, more enthusiasm and tenderness, who has a greater knowledge of human nature, and a more comprehensive soul, than are supposed to be common among mankind; a man pleased with his own passions and volitions, and who rejoices more than other men in the spirit of life that is in him; delighting to contemplate similar volitions and passions as manifested in the goings-on of the Universe, and habitually impelled to create them where he does not find them. To these qualities he has added a disposition to be affected more than other men by absent things as if they were present; an ability of conjuring up in himself passions, which are indeed far from being the same as those produced by real events, yet (especially in those parts of the general sympathy which are pleasing and delightful) do more nearly resemble the passions produced by real events, than any thing which, from the motions of their own minds merely, other men are accustomed to feel in themselves; whence, and from practice, he has acquired a greater readiness and power in expressing what he thinks and feels, and especially those thoughts and feelings which, by his own choice, or from the structure of his own mind, arise in him without immediate external excitement.

But, whatever portion of this faculty we may suppose even the greatest Poet to possess, there cannot be a doubt but that the language which it will suggest to him, must, in liveliness and truth, fall far short of that which is uttered by men in real life, under the actual pressure of those passions, certain shadows of which the Poet thus produces, or feels to be produced, in himself. However exalted a notion we would wish to cherish of the character of a Poet, it is obvious, that, while he describes and imitates passions, his situation is altogether slavish and mechanical, compared with the freedom and power of real and substantial action and suffering. So that it will be the wish of the Poet to bring his feelings near to those of the persons whose feelings he describes, nay, for short spaces of time perhaps, to let himself slip into an entire delusion, and even confound and identify his own feelings with theirs; modifying only the language which is thus suggested to him, by a consideration that he describes for a particular purpose, that of giving pleasure. Here, then, he will apply the principle on which I have so much insisted, namely, that of selection; on this he will depend for removing what would otherwise be painful or disgusting in the passion; he will feel that there is no necessity to trick out or to elevate nature: and, the more industriously he applies this principle, the deeper will be his faith that no words, which his fancy or imagination can suggest, will be to be compared with those which are the emanations of reality and truth.

But it may be said by those who do not object to the general spirit of these remarks, that, as it is impossible for the Poet to produce upon all occasions language as exquisitely fitted for the passion as that which the real passion itself suggests, it is proper that he should consider himself as in the situation of a translator, who deems himself justified when he substitutes excellences of another kind for those which are unattainable by him; and endeavours occasionally to surpass his original, in order to make some amends for the general inferiority to which he feels that he must submit. But this would be to encourage idleness and unmanly despair. Further, it is the language of men who speak of what they do not understand; who talk of Poetry as of a matter of amusement and idle pleasure; who will converse with us as gravely about a *taste* for Poetry, as they express it, as if it were a thing as indifferent as a taste for Rope-dancing, or Frontiniac or Sherry. Aristotle, I have been told, hath said, that Poetry is the most philosophic of all writing: it is so: its object is truth, not individual and local, but general, and operative; not standing upon external testimony, but carried alive into the heart by passion; truth which is its own testimony, which gives strength and divinity to the tribunal to which it appeals, and receives them from the same tribunal. Poetry is the image of man and nature. The obstacles which stand in the way of the fidelity of the Biographer and Historian, and of their consequent utility, are incalculably greater than those which are to be encountered by the Poet who has an adequate notion of the dignity of his art. The Poet writes under one restriction only, namely, that of the necessity of giving immediate pleasure to a human Being possessed of that information which may be expected from him, not as a lawyer, a physician, a mariner, an astronomer or a natural philosopher, but as a Man. Except this one restriction, there is no object standing between the Poet and the image of things; between this, and the Biographer and Historian there are a thousand.

Nor let this necessity of producing immediate pleasure be considered as a degradation of the Poet's art. It is far otherwise. It is an acknowledgment of the beauty of the universe, an acknowledgment the more sincere because it is not formal, but indirect; it is a task light and easy to him who looks at the world in the spirit of love: further, it is a homage paid to the native and naked dignity of man, to the grand elementary principle of pleasure, by which he knows, and feels, and lives, and moves. We have no sympathy but what is propagated by pleasure: I would not be misunderstood; but wherever we sympathize with pain it will be found that the sympathy is produced and carried on by subtle combinations with pleasure. We have no knowledge, that is, no general principles drawn from the contemplation of particular facts, but what has been built up by pleasure, and exists in us by pleasure alone. The Man of Science, the Chemist and Mathematician, whatever difficulties and disgusts they may have had to struggle with, know and feel this. However painful may be the objects with which the Anatomist's knowledge is connected, he feels that his knowledge is pleasure; and where he has no pleasure he has no knowledge. What then does the Poet? He considers man and the objects that surround him as acting and re-acting upon each other, so as to produce an infinite complexity of pain and pleasure; he considers man in his own nature and in his ordinary life as contemplating this with a certain quantity of immediate knowledge, with certain convictions, intuitions, and deductions which by habit become of the nature of intuitions; he considers him as looking upon this complex scene of ideas and sensations, and finding every where objects that immediately excite in him sympathies which, from the necessities of his nature, are accompanied by an overbalance of enjoyment.

To this knowledge which all men carry about with them, and to these sympathies in which without any other discipline than that of our daily life we are fitted to take delight, the Poet principally directs his attention. He considers man and nature as essentially adapted to each other, and the mind of man as naturally the mirror of the fairest and most interesting qualities of nature. And thus the Poet, prompted by this feeling of pleasure which accompanies him through the whole course of his studies, converses with general nature with affections akin to those, which, through labour and length of time, the Man of Science has raised up in himself, by conversing with those particular parts of nature which are the objects of his studies. The knowledge both of the Poet and the Man of Science is pleasure; but the knowledge of the one cleaves to us as a necessary part of our existence, our natural and unalienable inheritance; the other is a personal and individual acquisition, slow to come to us, and by no habitual and direct sympathy connecting us with our fellow-beings. The Man of Science seeks truth as a remote and unknown benefactor; he cherishes and loves it in his solitude: the Poet, singing a song in which all human beings join with him, rejoices in the presence of truth as our visible friend and hourly companion. Poetry is the breath and finer spirit of all knowledge; it is the impassioned expression which is in the countenance of all Science. Emphatically may it be said of the Poet, as Shakespeare hath said of man, 'that he looks before and after.' He is the rock of defence of human nature; an upholder and preserver, carrying every where with him relationship and love. In spite of difference of soil and climate, of language and manners, of laws and customs, in spite of things silently gone out of mind and things violently destroyed, the Poet binds together by passion and knowledge the vast empire of human society, as it is spread over the whole earth, and over all time. The objects of the Poet's thoughts are every where; though the eyes and senses of man are, it is true, his favorite guides, yet he will follow wheresoever he can find an atmosphere of sensation in which to move his wings. Poetry is the first and last of all knowledge – it is as immortal as the heart of man. If the labours of men of Science should ever create any material revolution, direct or indirect, in our condition, and in the impressions which we habitually receive, the Poet will sleep then no more than at present, but he will be ready to follow the steps of the man of Science, not only in those general indirect effects, but he will be at his side, carrying sensation into the midst of the objects of the Science itself. The remotest discoveries of the Chemist, the Botanist, or Mineralogist, will be as proper objects of the Poet's art as any upon which it can be employed, if the time should ever come when these things shall be familiar to us, and the relations under which they are contemplated by the followers of these respective Sciences shall be manifestly and palpably material to us as enjoying and suffering beings. If the time should ever come when what is now called Science, thus familiarized to men, shall be ready to put on, as it were, a form of flesh and blood, the Poet will lend his divine spirit to aid the transfiguration, and will welcome the Being thus produced, as a dear and genuine inmate of the household of man. – It is not, then, to be supposed that any one, who holds that sublime notion of Poetry which I have attempted to convey, will break in upon the sanctity and truth of his pictures by transitory and accidental ornaments, and endeavour to excite admiration of himself by arts, the necessity of which must manifestly depend upon the assumed meanness of his subject.

What I have thus far said applies to Poetry in general; but especially to those parts of composition where the Poet speaks through the mouths of his characters; and upon this point it appears to have such weight that I will conclude, there are few persons, of good sense, who would not allow that the dramatic parts of composition are defective, in proportion as they deviate from the real language of nature, and are coloured by a diction of the Poet's own, either peculiar to him as an individual Poet, or belonging simply to Poets in general, to a body of men who, from the circumstance of their compositions being in metre, it is expected will employ a particular language.

It is not, then, in the dramatic parts of composition that we look for this distinction of language; but still it may be proper and necessary when the Poet speaks to us in his own person and character. To this I answer by referring my Reader to the description which I have before given of a Poet. Among the qualities which I have enumerated as principally conducing to form a Poet, is implied nothing differing in kind from other men, but only in degree. The sum of what I have there said is, that the Poet is chiefly distinguished from other men by a greater promptness to think and feel without immediate external excitement, and a greater power in expressing such thoughts and feelings as are produced in him in that manner. But these passions and thoughts and feelings are the general passions and thoughts and feelings of men. And with what are they connected? Undoubtedly with our moral sentiments and animal sensations, and with the causes which excite these; with the operations of the elements and the appearances of the visible universe; with storm and sun-shine, with the revolutions of the seasons, with cold and heat, with loss of friends and kindred, with injuries and resentments, gratitude and hope, with fear and sorrow. These, and the like, are the sensations and objects which the Poet describes, as they are the sensations of other men, and the objects which interest them. The Poet thinks and feels in the spirit of the passions of men. How, then, can his language differ in any material degree from that of all other men who feel vividly and see clearly? It might be *proved* that it is impossible. But supposing that this were not the case, the Poet might then be allowed to use a peculiar language, when expressing his feelings for his own gratification, or that of men like himself. But Poets do not write for Poets alone, but for men. Unless therefore we are advocates for that admiration which depends upon ignorance, and that pleasure which arises from hearing what we do not understand, the Poet must descend from this supposed height, and, in order to excite rational sympathy, he must express himself as other men express themselves. To this it may be added, that while he is only selecting from the real language of men, or, which amounts to the same thing, composing accurately in the spirit of such selection, he is treading upon safe ground, and we know what we are to expect from him. Our feelings are the same with respect to metre; for, as it may be proper to remind the Reader, [...the distinction of rhyme and metre is uniform ...] [the sentence then continues as in the first edition].

Chapter XIV from Coleridge's *Biographia Literaria* (1817)

Occasion of the Lyrical Ballads, and the objects originally proposed – Preface to the second edition – The ensuing controversy, its causes and acrimony – Philosophic definitions of a Poem and Poetry, with scholia.

During the first year that Mr Wordsworth and I were neighbours, our conversations turned frequently on the two cardinal points of poetry, the power of exciting the sympathy of the reader by a faithful adherence to the truth of nature, and the power of giving the interest of novelty by the modifying colours of imagination. The sudden charm, which accidents of light and shade, which moonlight or sunset, diffused over a known and familiar landscape, appeared to represent the practicability of combining both. These are the poetry of nature. The thought suggested itself (to which of us I do not recollect) that a series of poems might be composed of two sorts. In the one, the incidents and agents were to be, in part at least, supernatural; and the excellence aimed at was to consist in the interesting of the affections by the dramatic truth of such emotions, as would naturally accompany such situations, supposing them real. And real in this sense they have been to every human being who, from whatever source of delusion, has at any time believed himself under supernatural agency. For the second class, subjects were to be chosen from ordinary life; the characters and incidents were to be such as will be found in every village and its vicinity where there is a meditative and feeling mind to seek after them, or to notice them, when they present themselves.

Chapter XIV from Coleridge's Biographia Literaria *(1817)*

In this idea originated the plan of the 'Lyrical Ballads'; in which it was agreed that my endeavours should be directed to persons and characters supernatural, or at least romantic; yet so as to transfer from our inward nature a human interest and a semblance of truth sufficient to procure for these shadows of imagination that willing suspension of disbelief for the moment, which constitutes poetic faith. Mr Wordsworth, on the other hand, was to propose to himself as his object, to give the charm of novelty to things of every day, and to excite a feeling analogous to the supernatural, by awakening the mind's attention from the lethargy of custom, and directing it to the loveliness and the wonders of the world before us; an inexhaustible treasure, but for which, in consequence of the film of familiarity and selfish solicitude, we have eyes, yet see not, ears that hear not, and hearts that neither feel nor understand.

With this view I wrote the 'Ancient Mariner,' and was preparing, among other poems, the 'Dark Ladie,' and the 'Christabel,' in which I should have more nearly realized my ideal, than I had done in my first attempt. But Mr Wordsworth's industry had proved so much more successful, and the number of his poems so much greater, that my compositions, instead of forming a balance, appeared rather an interpolation of heterogeneous matter. Mr Wordsworth added two or three poems written in his own character, in the impassioned, lofty, and sustained diction which is characteristic of his genius. In this form the 'Lyrical Ballads' were published; and were presented by him as an experiment, whether subjects, which from their nature rejected the usual ornaments and extra-colloquial style of poems in general, might not be so managed in the language of ordinary life as to produce the pleasurable interest which it is the peculiar business of poetry to impart. To the second edition he added a preface of considerable length; in which, notwithstanding some passages of apparently a contrary import, he was understood to contend for the extension of this style to poetry of all kinds, and to reject as vicious and indefensible all phrases and forms of style that were not included in what he (unfortunately, I think, adopting an equivocal expression) called the language of real life. From this preface, prefixed to poems in which it was impossible to deny the presence of original genius, however mistaken its direction might be deemed, arose the whole long-continued controversy. For from the conjunction of perceived power with supposed heresy I explain the inveteracy, and in some instances, I grieve to say, the acrimonious passions, with which the controversy has been conducted by the assailants.

Had Mr Wordsworth's poems been the silly, the childish things, which they were for a long time described as being; had they been really distinguished from the compositions of other poets merely by meanness of language and inanity of thought; had they indeed contained nothing more than what is found in the parodies and pretended imitations of them; they must have sunk at once, a dead weight, into the slough of oblivion, and have dragged the preface along with them. But year after year increased the number of Mr Wordsworth's admirers. They were found, too, not in the lower classes of the reading public, but chiefly among young men of strong ability and meditative minds; and their admiration (inflamed perhaps in some degree by opposition) was distinguished by its intensity, I might almost say, by its religious fervour. These facts, and the intellectual energy of the author, which was more or less consciously felt, where it was outwardly and even boisterously denied, meeting with sentiments of aversion to his opinions, and of alarm at their consequences, produced an eddy of criticism, which would of itself have borne up the poems by the violence with which it whirled them round and round. With many parts of this preface, in the sense attributed to them, and which the words undoubtedly seem to authorize, I never concurred; but, on the contrary, objected to them as erroneous in principle, and as contradictory (in appearance at least) both to other parts of the same preface and to the author's own practice in the greater number of the poems themselves. Mr Wordsworth, in his recent collection, has, I find, degraded this prefatory disquisition to the end of his second volume, to be read or not at the reader's choice. But he has not, as far as I can discover, announced any change in his poetic creed. At all events, considering it as the source of a controversy, in which I have been honoured more than I deserve by the frequent conjunction of my name with his, I think it expedient to declare, once for all, in what points I coincide with his opinions, and in what points I altogether differ. But in order to render myself intelligible I must previously, in as few words as possible, explain my ideas, first, of a poem; and secondly, of poetry itself, in kind and in essence.

The office of philosophical disquisition consists in just distinction; while it is the privilege of the philosopher to preserve himself constantly aware, that distinction is not division. In order to obtain adequate notions of any truth, we must intellectually separate its distinguishable parts; and this is the technical process of philosophy. But having so done, we must then restore them in our conceptions to the unity in which they actually co-exist; and this is the result of philosophy. A poem contains the same elements as a prose composition; the difference, therefore, must consist in a different combination of them, in consequence of a different object proposed. According to the difference of the object will be the difference of the combination. It is possible that the object may be merely to facilitate the recollection of any given facts or observations by artificial arrangement; and the composition will be a poem, merely because it is distinguished from composition in prose by metre, or by rhyme, or by both conjointly. In this, the lowest sense, a man might attribute the name of a poem to the well-known enumeration of the days in the several months:

'Thirty days hath September,
April, June, and November,' &c.

and others of the same class and purpose. And as a particular pleasure is found in anticipating the recurrence of sounds and quantities, all compositions that have this charm superadded, whatever be their contents, *may* be entitled poems.

255

So much for the superficial form. A difference of object and contents supplies an additional ground of distinction. The immediate purpose may be the communication of truths; either of truth absolute and demonstrable, as in works of science; or of facts experienced and recorded, as in history. Pleasure, and that of the highest and most permanent kind, may result from the attainment of the end; but it is not itself the Blest indeed is that state of society, in which the immediate purpose would be baffled by the perversion of the proper ultimate end; in which no charm of diction or imagery could exempt the Bathyllus even of an Anacreon, or the Alexis of Virgil, from disgust and aversion!

But the communication of pleasure may be the immediate object of a work not metrically composed; and that object may have been in a high degree attained, as in novels and romances. Would then the mere superaddition of metre, with or without rhyme, entitle these to the name of poems? The answer is, that nothing can permanently please, which does not contain in itself the reason why it is so, and not otherwise. If metre be superadded, all other parts must be made consonant with it. They must be such as to justify the perpetual and distinct attention to each part, which an exact correspondent recurrence of accent and sound are calculated to excite. The final definition then, so deduced, may be thus worded. A poem is that species of composition, which is opposed to works of science, by proposing for its immediate object pleasure, not truth; and from all other species (having this object in common with it) it is discriminated by proposing to itself such delight from the whole, as is compatible with a distinct gratification from each component part.

Controversy is not seldom excited in consequence of the disputants attaching each a different meaning to the same word; and in few instances has this been more striking than in disputes concerning the present subject. If a man chooses to call every composition a poem, which is rhyme, or measure, or both, I must leave his opinion uncontroverted. The distinction is at least competent to characterize the writer's intention. If it were subjoined, that the whole is likewise entertaining or affecting, as a tale, or as a series of interesting reflections, I of course admit this as another fit ingredient of a poem, and an additional merit. But if the definition sought for be that of a legitimate poem, I answer, it must be one the parts of which mutually support and explain each other; all in their proportion harmonizing with, and supporting the purpose and known influences of metrical arrangement. The philosophic critics of all ages coincide with the ultimate judgment of all countries, in equally denying the praises of a just poem, on the one hand to a series of striking lines or distichs, each of which absorbing the whole attention of the reader to itself, disjoins it from its context, and makes it a separate whole, instead of an harmonizing part; and on the other hand, to an unsustained composition, from which the reader collects rapidly the general result unattracted by the component parts. The reader should be carried forward, not merely or chiefly by the mechanical impulse of curiosity, or by a restless desire to arrive at the final solution; but by the pleasurable activity of mind excited by the attractions of the journey itself. Like the motion of a serpent, which the Egyptians made the emblem of intellectual power; or like the path of sound through the air; at every step he pauses and half recedes, and from the retrogressive movement collects the force which again carries him onward. *Precipitandus est liber spiritus*, says Petronius Arbiter most happily. The epithet, *liber*, here balances the preceding verb: and it is not easy to conceive more meaning condensed in fewer words.

But if this should be admitted as a satisfactory character of a poem, we have still to seek for a definition of poetry. The writings of Plato, and Bishop Taylor, and the *Theoria Sacra* of Burnet, furnish undeniable proofs that poetry of the highest kind may exist without metre, and even without the contradistinguishing objects of a poem. The first chapter of Isaiah (indeed a very large proportion of the whole book) is poetry in the most emphatic sense; yet it would be not less irrational than strange to assert, that pleasure, and not truth, was the immediate object of the prophet. In short, whatever specific import we attach to the word poetry, there, will be found involved in it, as a necessary consequence, that a poem of any length neither can be, nor ought to be, all poetry. Yet if a harmonious whole is to be produced, the remaining parts must be preserved in keeping with the poetry; and this can be no otherwise effected than by such a studied selection and artificial arrangement as will partake of one, though not a peculiar, property of poetry. And this again can be no other than the property of exciting a more continuous and equal attention than the language of prose aims at, whether colloquial or written.

My own conclusions on the nature of poetry, in the strictest use of the word, have been in part anticipated in the preceding disquisition on the fancy and imagination. What is poetry? is so nearly the same question with, what is a poem? that the answer to the one is involved in the solution of the other. For it is a distinction resulting from the poetic genius itself, which sustains and modifies the images, thoughts, and emotions of the poet's own mind. A poet, described in ideal perfection, brings the whole soul of man into activity, with the subordination of its faculties to each other, according to their relative worth and dignity. He diffuses a tone, and spirit of unity, that blends, and (as it were) fuses, each into each, by that synthetic and magical power to which we have exclusively appropriated the name of imagination. This power, first put in action by the will and understanding, and retained under their irremissive, though gentle and unnoticed, control (*laxis effertur habenis*) reveals itself in the balance or reconciliation of opposite or discordant qualities: of sameness, with difference; of the general, with the concrete; the idea, with the image; the individual, with the representative; the sense of novelty and freshness, with old and familiar objects; a more than usual state of emotion, with more than usual order; judgment ever awake and steady self-possession, with enthusiasm and feeling profound or vehement; and while it blends and harmonizes the natural and the artificial, still subordinates art to nature; the manner to the matter; and our admiration of the poet to our sympathy with the poetry.

Chapter XIV from Coleridge's Biographia Literaria *(1817)*

'Doubtless,' as Sir John Davies observes of the soul (and his words may with slight alteration be applied, and even more appropriately, to the poetic imagination) –

> Doubtless this could not be, but that she turns
> Bodies to spirit by sublimation strange,
> As fire converts to fire the things it burns,
> As we our food into our nature change.
>
> From their gross matter she abstracts their forms,
> And draws a kind of quintessence from things,
> Which to her proper nature she transforms
> To bear them light, on her celestial wings.
>
> Thus does she, when from individual states
> She doth abstract the universal kinds;
> Which then re-clothed in divers names and fates
> Steal access through our senses to our minds.

Finally, good sense is the body of poetic genius, fancy its drapery, motion its life, and imagination the soul that is everywhere, and in each; and forms all into one graceful and intelligent whole.

(Source: Samuel Taylor Coleridge, *Biographia Literaria and Two Lay Sermons*, George Bell & Sons, 1898)

Further Reading

The following texts are a combination of specialist and general reading.

M.H. Abrams (ed.), *Wordsworth: A Collection of Critical Essays*, Spectrum (Twentieth Century Views), 1972. Spans a wide range of opinions from different periods and considers two different views, the complex and the simple.

Owen Barfield, *What Coleridge Thought* (Wesleyan University Press, 1971). A scholarly and imaginative examination of Coleridge's philosophy of contraries, and of the German background.

Marilyn Butler, *Romantics, Rebels and Reactionaries: English Literature and its Background 1760–1830* (Oxford University Press, 1981). A good general introduction to the effects of political change.

A.S. Byatt, *Unruly Times: Wordsworth and Coleridge in their Times* (Vintage, 1997). A novelist's rather than a critic's view of the period.

Stephen Gill (ed.), *William Wordsworth: A Life* (Clarendon Press, 1989). A detailed biography. Also *Wordsworth and the Victorians* (Clarendon Press, 2001). Excellent on Wordsworth's changing critical fortunes.

John O. Hayden (ed.), *William Wordsworth: Selected Prose* (Penguin, 1988). Considers the prose writings, including the Preface, supported by detailed notes.

Richard Holmes, *Coleridge: Early Visions* (Hodder & Stoughton, 1989), and *Coleridge: Darker Reflections* (HarperCollins, 1998). Eminently readable biography; slightly biased against Wordsworth.

Further Reading

John Livingstone Lowes, *The Road to Xanadu* (Picador, 1978). A massive survey of Coleridge's reading based on the Notebooks of 1795–1800 and their relation to his major poems.

Iain McCalman (ed.), *An Oxford Companion to the Romantic Age, 1776–1832* (Oxford University Press, 1999).

Jerome J. McGann, *The Poetics of Sensibility: A Revolution in Style* (Oxford University Press, 1999).

Lucy Newlyn (General editor), *The Cambridge Companion to Coleridge* (Cambridge University Press, 2002). Recent articles on a range of subjects including politics, poetry, notebooks, and conversation. James Engell's essay on *Biographia Literaria* is particularly useful.